# M10 TANK DESTROYER
## vs
# StuG III ASSAULT GUN

### Germany 1944

STEVEN J. ZALOGA

First published in Great Britain in 2013 by Osprey Publishing,
Midland House, West Way, Botley, Oxford, OX2 0PH, UK
43-01 21st Street, Suite 220B, Long Island City, NY 11101
E-mail: info@ospreypublishing.com

Osprey Publishing is part of the Osprey Group

A CIP catalog record for this book is available from the British Library

Print ISBN: 978 1 78096 099 9
PDF ebook ISBN: 978 1 78096 100 2
ePub ebook ISBN: 978 1 78096 101 9

Index by Mark Swift
Typeset in ITC Conduit and Adobe Garamond
Maps by bounford.com
Originated by PDQ Media, Bungay, UK
Printed in China through Asia Pacific Offset Limited

13 14 15 16 17   10 9 8 7 6 5 4 3 2 1

Osprey Publishing is supporting the Woodland Trust, the UK's leading
woodland conservation charity, by funding the dedication of trees.

www.ospreypublishing.com

**Key to military symbols**

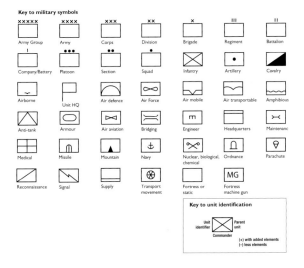

**Author's note**

The author would like to thank Timm Haasler and Richard Hedrick of
www.sturmpanzer.com for their generous research help on this project.
Thanks also go the staff of Military Vehicle Technology Museum in Portola
Valley, California, for their help while photographing their superbly restored
StuG III Ausf G.

For brevity, the traditional conventions have been used when referring to
units. In the case of US units, 2/119th Infantry refers to the 2nd Battalion,
119th Infantry Regiment. The US Army traditionally uses Arabic numerals
for divisions and smaller independent formations (70th Division, 781st Tank
Battalion); Roman numerals for corps (VI Corps), spelled-out numbers for
field armies (First US Army); and Arabic numerals for army groups
(12th Army Group).

In the case of German units, 2./Pz-Rgt 7 refers to the 2. Kompanie, Panzer-
Regiment Nr. 7; II./Pz-Rgt 7 indicates the II. Abteilung, Panzer-Regiment
Nr. 7. German corps have two accepted forms, the formal version using
Roman numerals (LXXXI. Armeekorps) and the shortened style using Arabic
(81.AK); the former has been used here. Likewise, the German field armies are
contracted in the usual fashion, (e.g. AOK 7 for Armeeoberkommando Nr. 7,
or Seventh Army). There are a variety of abbreviations for assault-gun brigades
such as Stu.Gesch.Brig., and the simpler StuG-Brig has been used here.

Photograph sources for this book include NARA (US National Archives and
Records Administration); MHI (Military History Institute, Army Historical
Education Center); and LAC (Library and Archives Canada).

**Editor's note**

All German measurements are given in metric (with weights in kilograms), with
conversions in US customary appended in parentheses. All US measurements
are given in US customary units (with weights given in US (short) tons,
pounds, and ounces). US customary measurements are employed in the
text for all measurements except for ammunition and armor, both of which
are expressed in metric; the Germans used centimeters rather than millimeters
for guns of 20mm and above.

**Conversions**

For ease of comparison please refer to the following conversion table:

1 mile = 1.6km
1yd = 0.9m
1ft = 0.3m
1in = 2.54cm/25.4mm
1 gallon (US) = 3.8 liters
1 ton (US) = 907kg
1lb = 0.45kg

# CONTENTS

# INTRODUCTION

The use of tanks for the close support of infantry units was one of the most controversial tactical dilemmas of World War II. Germany's Blitzkrieg victories in Poland in 1939 and France in 1940 suggested that tanks should be concentrated in armored divisions and that none should be diverted to infantry support at the small-unit level. Yet the Wehrmacht itself soon learned the value of specialized infantry-support armored fighting vehicles (AFV), both in the form of the tank destroyer (Panzerjäger) and assault gun (Sturmgeschütz). By 1944, more than a quarter of German AFVs were committed to the infantry-support role, and by the end of the war, they were the majority in some theaters. This book explores this tactical conundrum by pitting two of the pre-eminent AFVs against each other in combat, the German StuG III assault gun and the American M10 tank destroyer. The encounter that serves as the focus of this book took place in early October 1944 on Germany's western border near Aachen, when the US XIX Corps attempted to penetrate the Scharnhorst Line that was being defended by the German LXXXI. Armeekorps.

The StuG III and the M10 3in Gun Motor Carriage (GMC) may seem an odd combination for consideration in the Duel series since they were designed for different tactical roles. The StuG III was originally developed as an assault gun for direct infantry support, while the M10 was developed as a tank destroyer to combat the Panzer force. Yet the StuG III gradually evolved into one of the Wehrmacht's most effective tank destroyers on the Eastern Front, and the M10 was often used in the assault-gun role by the US Army in the European Theater of Operations (ETO). By 1944, they had both evolved into multipurpose AFVs and were used to provide armored support for infantry units.

Neither vehicle has attracted as much attention as the more famous Tiger, Panther, and Sherman. Yet the StuG III was one of the most widely produced German AFVs

of World War II. Although it started the war as a relatively minor type, by 1944–45 it often outnumbered the PzKpfw IV and Panther on the battlefield. The M10 was a specialized derivative of the famous Sherman tank. It saw extensive combat use starting in Tunisia in 1943, and on through Sicily, Italy, and Northwest Europe, and even in the Pacific and on the Eastern Front.

The StuG III and M10 were developed to provide alternative tactical approaches to the early tactics of Blitzkrieg warfare. In the late 1930s, the Heer (German Army) had originally intended to provide its infantry divisions with armored support. However, German industry was slow in providing enough tanks for the new Panzer divisions, and so the army concentrated its AFVs in these units. This stood in considerable contrast to other armies of the Great Powers such as France, Britain, and the Soviet Union, which traditionally divided their tank force between the infantry-support tank units and the cavalry/armored force. Germany's stunning defeat of France in 1940 and the decisive role of the Panzer force in this victory convinced many observers that the traditional bifurcation of the AFV force into infantry/cavalry roles was a mistake. This was especially the case in the United States, which was on the verge of creating a massive new armored force and was looking for a model on which to base its future configuration. The US Army's armored divisions were patterned on the Panzer force, but the tank-destroyer concept emerged in 1940 as a distinctly American answer to the Panzer threat. As will be described in more detail below, this proved to be the wrong answer to the wrong tactical question.

Yet the concentration of the Panzer force in 1940 proved to be a temporary fluke. German commanders quickly appreciated Marshal Philippe Pétain's famous quote from the 1918 fighting: "There are two kinds of infantry: men who have gone into action with tanks, and men who have not; and the former never want to go into action

The principal role for the StuG III was infantry support. This is a StuG III Ausf F of 1./StuG-Abt 210 during the fighting in the Kuban in southern Russia in the fall of 1942. (NARA)

without tanks again." The modern battlefield had become a very dangerous place for the rifleman, and armored support provided a vital ingredient in restoring the offensive capability of the infantry in the face of enemy machine guns, fortifications, and tanks. German commanders had never doubted that infantry-support tanks would be valuable, but they did face the dilemma of how to produce enough AFVs to satisfy both the needs of the Panzer divisions and the infantry. The solution came in the form of a low-cost tank substitute, namely the turretless Sturmgeschütz (StuG) assault gun. This weapon began to appear in tiny numbers in 1940. By the time of the 1941 invasion of the USSR, only about 400 were in service. The StuG III became so popular in the infantry divisions that production continued to expand, from barely 50 per month in 1941 to more than 500 a month in 1944, a ten-fold increase. As the numbers on the Eastern Front continued to grow, so did the StuG III's tactical role. The early StuG III was armed with a short 7.5cm gun that had very poor antitank performance. Yet it quickly became apparent that the numerous Soviet tanks represented a persistent threat to the German infantry. As a result, new versions with the long 7.5cm guns began to appear in 1942, and the StuG III gradually evolved into a dual-purpose weapon, both for close fire support of the infantry against unarmored targets, as well as a potent antitank weapon.

In the case of the M10, the process was completely the reverse. Although it had been intended primarily as a method to combat German Panzer divisions, when the M10 was first deployed in Tunisia in 1943, the Panzer threat had evolved. Massed attacks by entire Panzer corps were a thing of the past, at least in the West, and German tanks tended to appear on the battlefield in much more dispersed formations. The performance of US Army tank destroyers in Tunisia in 1943 was so uninspiring that none were deployed in the invasion of Sicily in July 1943. Although they were used in growing numbers in Italy in 1943–44, encounters with German AFVs were so infrequent that new missions were sought. The M10 ended up being attached to infantry units to provide direct-fire support, and it was also seconded to divisional artillery in some campaigns to deepen its firepower for key indirect-fire missions. Instead of being a dedicated tank destroyer, the M10 gradually evolved into being a multipurpose assault gun, most often used for infantry support. A report by the commander of the US 5th Tank Destroyer (TD) Group in Normandy in 1944 reiterated Pétain's maxim:

> What is not in the field manuals on tank destroyer use is the effective support that they render to a fighting infantry at the time of actual combat. An infantryman has his fortitude well tested and the mere presence of self-propelled tank destroyers in his immediate vicinity gives a tremendous shot of courage to the committed infantryman. For example, at Chambois during the closing of the Falaise Gap in August 1944, an infantry battalion moved towards the town with utter fearlessness to enemy artillery, mortar, and small arms fire when accompanied by some M10s. However, the M10s were delayed in crossing a stream for about thirty-five minutes. During this time, the infantry battalion continued to their objective, which dominated a roadway leading to Chambois. They fought infantry, they bazooka-ed some armored vehicles including three tanks on the road, but on realizing that the M10s weren't firing, they started a retirement. Leading the parade to the rear was a short lad known as "Shorty." Shorty in the lead was the first

man to see a platoon of M10s who had finally gotten across the stream. Shorty took a good look at the M10s, turned around, and shouted to the other me "Hell boys, what are we retiring for, here comes the TDs!" The entire company in mass immediately reversed their direction and returned to their excellent positions, and to say they fought for the next few hours with unusual bravery is stating it mildly. The point I am trying to make is that the appearance and the knowledge that self-propelled tank-destroyers were at hand was a major reason that the infantry attained success and victory. Often many men die or suffer to retain or exploit IF the inspiration furnished by the presence of self-propelled tank destroyers is known. The towed guns can be just as brave and thoroughly trained, but they never give much "oomph" to the fighting doughboy when the chips are really down.

The German infantry commanders, especially those on the Eastern Front, strongly agreed with this sentiment. The StuG III was often described as a "rock among the waves," a vital mobile strongpoint to bolster the embattled German infantryman. It was frequently called "the backbone of the infantry."

As a result of the twists and turns in the evolution of AFV technology and tactics, by the time the M10 and the StuG III faced one another in the ETO in June 1944, they were being used in a very similar fashion for infantry support even if they bore little technical resemblance. The underlying theme of this book is the tactical adaptation of AFVs in World War II that occurred due to evolving battlefield tactics in spite of the awkward fit of their technical features to their new tactical missions.

# CHRONOLOGY

**1936**

**June** — Development contract for Sturmgeschütz awarded to Daimler-Benz.

**1940**

**January** — First series-production StuG III completed.

**May** — Combat debut of StuG III during campaign in France and the Low Countries.

**1941**

**November** — Development of 3in tank destroyer on M4 medium-tank chassis begins.

**1942**

**February** — Completion of last StuG III Ausf E with short L/24 gun; first StuG III Ausf F with L/43 gun.

**April** — T35 and T35E1 pilots delivered to Aberdeen Proving Grounds, Maryland, for trials.

**June** — M10 3in GMC accepted for US Army service.

**June** — Frontal armor of StuG III increased to 80mm.

**December** — First production of StuG III Ausf G.

**1943**

**January** — Production of M10 with intermediate wedge-shaped counterweight begins.

**February** — StuG III production begins at MIAG in Braunschweig; StuH 42 begins series production.

**March** — Production of definitive M10 and M10A1 with "duck-bill" counterweight begins.

A classic image of an M10 of the 801st TD Battalion on an infantry-support assignment with the 3/22nd Infantry (4th Division) near Mabompré, Belgium on September 8, 1944. It was common US Army practice to load up infantry on available armored vehicles during rapid pursuit operations to create a mechanized task force. (NARA)

A StuG III Ausf G named "Sperber" (sparrow hawk) of StuG-Brig 202, which fought in the Kurland region of the Baltic in the late summer and fall of 1944. This is from Alkett's May–June 1944 production batch. Some units mounted the rear maintenance hatches on the bow for extra armor as seen here. (Author's collection)

| | |
|---|---|
| **March 23** | Combat debut of M10 at battle of El Guettar in Tunisia. |

## 1944

| | |
|---|---|
| **October 2** | The XIX Corps of the First US Army begins attacks towards Übach-Palenberg to penetrate Scharnhorst Line north of Aachen. |
| **October 3** | The 702nd TD Battalion and Combat Command B of the 2nd Armored Division begin to move over the Wurm River. |
| **October 3** | LXXXI. Armeekorps consolidates scattered assault-gun units as gepanzerte Gruppe Barkley to provide armored support for the 183. Volksgrenadier-Division counterattack. |
| **October 4** | Gruppe Barkley's assault guns support attack on Rimburg and force back Company I, 119th Infantry. |
| **October 5** | Failure of October 4 counterattacks forces AOK 7 to move more armored reinforcements into the Übach-Palenberg sector. |
| **October 6** | Heavy losses in Combat Command B force the 2nd Armored Division to commit Combat Command A as well. |
| **October 7** | Assault-gun strength in LXXXI. Armeekorps divided into two battle groups under the command of the 183. Volksgrenadier-Division and the 49. Infanterie-Division. |
| **October 8** | Assault guns supporting the 49. Infanterie-Division committed to a counterattack to regain Alsdorf. |
| **October 9** | Failure of the October 8 counterattack and activation of the US VII Corps south of Aachen force LXXXI. Armeekorps to redirect many assault guns back to the Aachen sector. |

# DESIGN AND DEVELOPMENT

## StuG III

### ORIGINS

The StuG III was the brainchild of Erich von Manstein, best known as the architect of the German victory over France in 1940, and one of Germany's premier field commanders during World War II. In 1935, he was an Oberst and served as the chief of the operations section of the general staff. Having been an infantryman in World War I, Manstein was all too familiar with the difficulty the infantry faced on the modern battlefield when advancing in the face of machine-gun nests and other defense works. While the field artillery could eventually destroy such obstacles, it took precious time to communicate from the front lines back to the field-gun batteries, and communications were often interrupted or delayed. The infantry needed some form of immediate and timely fire support, especially at critical moments during breakthrough operations. The short-term solution to this problem was the development of accompanying guns, small field guns that were light enough that they could be pushed forward by the infantry without the need of horses. These became a common feature in European armies of World War II, and each German infantry regiment had a gun company equipped with six of the small 7.5cm leIG 18 light infantry guns and two of the horse-drawn 15cm sIG 33 heavy infantry guns.

The StuG III was quite novel in 1940 and there was considerable need for tactical experimentation. This is a training exercise in Le Havre, France on September 24, 1940 with German infantry practicing with a StuG III for the planned invasion of Britain, Operation *Sealion*. (NARA)

While these guns were better than nothing, Manstein was well aware of the difficulty of moving them across shell-scarred terrain, and wanted a more modern type of Sturmartillerie, or assault artillery. The obvious solution was for a mobile and protected gun, and Manstein suggested that each infantry division receive an assault-gun battalion (Sturmgeschütz-Abteilung) with three batteries of six guns each. By centralizing the battalion under the division's control, the assault guns could be concentrated at the focal point (*Schwerpunkt*) of an offensive assault, or disperse a battery to each regiment in the event of defensive combat. Manstein won the support of the Heer commander-in-chief, Generaloberst Werner von Fritsch, and a development contract was awarded to Daimler-Benz in June 1936.

The StuG design became embroiled in politics after Fritsch was forced to resign in February 1938 following confrontations with Heinrich Himmler and other Nazi leaders who wanted a more politicized army leadership. The StuG concept lost its most critical supporter, while at the same time picking up an ardent opponent, Generalleutnant Heinz Guderian. By 1938, German tank production was at a turning point. The tank fighting in the Spanish Civil War (1936–39) made it clear that cheap machine-gun-armed tanks such as the PzKpfw I were ineffective, and that more armor was needed to defend tanks against the ubiquitous 37mm antitank guns. Guderian pressed for an expansion in the production of the new PzKpfw III medium tank, which he hoped would form the backbone of the new Panzer divisions. PzKpfw III production was still modest at this point, and it so happened that the Daimler-Benz StuG prototype was based precisely on this tank type. Guderian criticized Manstein and his supporters on the general staff, such as Generalmajor Walter Model, as "grave-diggers of the Panzer force" for trying to divert precious industrial resources away from the tanks in favor of infantry-support weapons. Germany's limited industrial capacity and the squabbling over the allocation of resources led the new Heer commander-in-chief, Generaloberst Walther von Brauchitsch, to downgrade Manstein's plans. Instead of a StuG battalion

# StuG III AUSF G, StuG-BRIG 394, OCTOBER 1944

22.21ft

in each infantry division, the new force would be limited to a smaller number of units, all assigned at field-army level. As a result of the delays, no assault-artillery units were ready in time for the 1939 invasion of Poland, and at the time of the invasion of France in May–June 1940, only four batteries were ready. Their performance in France was exceptional enough that permission was granted to expand the force as industrial resources became available.

The initial production version of the StuG III[1] was armed with a short 7.5cm cannon with a barrel length of L/24 calibers.[2] Only 95 of these were completed up to the beginning of 1941. While this weapon was perfectly adequate when dealing with non-armored targets, the fighting in the France campaign made it clear that enemy tanks would present a frequent threat to infantry attacks. Rheinmetall/Borsig had already developed a L/41 7.5cm gun, and it was experimentally mounted on a StuG III chassis in the winter of 1940/41. While the program had lower priority than guns intended for the tanks, the tank panic in the summer of 1941, caused by the unexpected appearance of the heavily armored Soviet T-34 and KV-1 tanks, led to greater interest in enhancing the Wehrmacht's antitank capabilities as quickly as possible. The new L/41 gun was modified into a slightly longer gun, the StuK 40 L/43, and was first fitted to the new StuG III Ausf F starting in February 1942.

---

1  The Wehrmacht used several different designations and abbreviations for these vehicles during the war; indeed the Muller/Zimmerman study has over a page devoted to the many changing designations. For simplicity's sake in this book, the abbreviation StuG III and StuH 42 are used for these two vehicles, although other designations may have been used at the time.

2  Barrel length is usually expressed in calibers, which are calculated by dividing the actual length of the gun tube by its diameter. So the initial StuG III gun was 1,800mm (70.9in) long with a 75mm (2.95in) diameter, and so L/24.

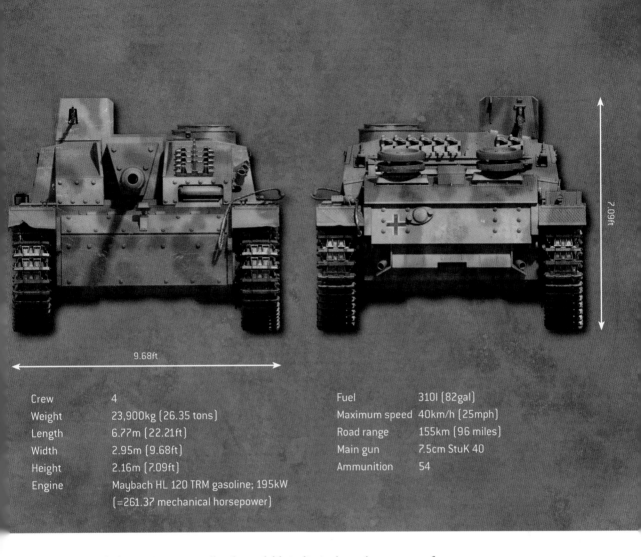

7.09ft

9.68ft

| | | | |
|---|---|---|---|
| Crew | 4 | Fuel | 310l (82gal) |
| Weight | 23,900kg (26.35 tons) | Maximum speed | 40km/h (25mph) |
| Length | 6.77m (22.21ft) | Road range | 155km (96 miles) |
| Width | 2.95m (9.68ft) | Main gun | 7.5cm StuK 40 |
| Height | 2.16m (7.09ft) | Ammunition | 54 |
| Engine | Maybach HL 120 TRM gasoline; 195kW (=261.37 mechanical horsepower) | | |

Even though the StuG III was still only available in limited numbers, reports from the Eastern Front were extremely positive about its role in reinforcing the infantry, and it attracted Hitler's personal enthusiasm. He began to see it as a critical ingredient in creating mobile pockets of resistance, and so he wanted it to be better protected with 80mm of frontal armor. This was accomplished at first by adding additional 30mm plates to the front starting in late June 1942, but by April 1943, the Alkett (Altmärkische Kettenwerk) plant near Berlin was building vehicles with 80mm frontal armor. Hitler also supported the enhancement of the StuG III's firepower, which paralleled the process on the PzKpfw IV tank with a new L/48 gun. The new StuG III Ausf G assault guns with the improved StuK 40 L/48 gun began to roll off the assembly lines in December 1942, and became the definitive version of the type.

The growing recognition of the value of the StuG III on the Eastern Front led to a continual increase in its production rate, with a corresponding increase in the number of assault-gun battalions. Production at the beginning of 1942 was only 45 per month, but by year's end this had nearly tripled to 120 per month. The StuG III received Hitler's critical favor due to numerous reports of its successes in Russia. Likewise, it was a very popular vehicle with the head of the German war industries, Albert Speer, since it was more economical of precious resources than comparable tanks. For example, the StuG III Ausf G cost only RM 82,500 while the PzKpfw III Ausf M cost RM 103,100 and the PzKpfw IV Ausf G cost RM 125,000. By this stage of the war, the PzKpfw III had become ineffective as a main battle tank, so StuG production could be increased by taking over these resources. As a result, when the "Adolf Hitler Armored Vehicle Program" was unveiled in September 1942 to increase Panzer production, StuG III production saw a substantial boost in resources, with the aim of increasing production to 300 per month by March 1944. In order to accommodate the increase, StuG production was extended from its main plant, Alkett, to the MIAG (Mühlenbau und Industrie Aktiengesellschaft) plant in Braunschweig in February 1943.

The StuH 42 assault gun closely resembled the standard StuG III Ausf G, but was fitted with the shorter 10.5cm howitzer. The early-production examples such as this one in Italy were fitted with a muzzle brake. This vehicle has the bolted 30mm appliqué on the superstructure front but already has the integral 80mm armor on the bow introduced at Alkett in April 1943. (NARA)

| StuG manufacture, 1940–45* | | | | | | | |
|---|---|---|---|---|---|---|---|
| | 1940 | 1941 | 1942 | 1943 | 1944 | 1945 | Total |
| StuG III L/24 | 183 | 541 | 90 | | | | 814 |
| StuG III L/43 | | | 118 | | | | 118 |
| StuG III L/48 | | | 571 | 2,934 | 3,894 | 863 | 8,262 |
| StuG IV | | | | 30 | 1,006 | 105 | 1,141 |
| StuH 42 | | | | 175 | 931 | 192 | 1,298 |
| Total | 183 | 541 | 779 | 3,139 | 5,831 | 1,160 | 11,633 |

*Monthly acceptances by the Waffenamt (Ordnance Office)

## STURMHAUBITZE 42

By late 1941, there had been discussions about increasing the firepower of the StuG III by substituting a 10.5cm leFH 18 in place of the 7.5cm gun. Due to the switch from the short L/24 7.5cm gun to the longer guns occurring in this period, however, the howitzer plan was put into limbo. The program was revived in late 1942 and the Sturmhaubitze (StuH 42) demonstrated to Hitler, who proved enthusiastic about the program. The infantry also voiced approval for the concept, since the gradual shift in focus in the StuG III armament towards weapons with better antitank performance tended to distort the use of the assault guns from general infantry fire-support to the antitank mission. At the same time, a variety of Panzerjäger were being put into production for the tank-destroyer role, so there was some

The later-production batches of the StuH 42 dispensed with the muzzle brake, as seen on this example from StuG-Brig 280 knocked out in the fighting in the Netherlands by the First Canadian Army in October 1944 in Woensdrecht. (LAC PA-137147)

interest in refocusing the StuG III to its original mission. The StuH 42 was not intended to replace the StuG, but rather to supplement it. In a standard 31-gun battalion, 22 were StuG and nine were StuH 42. Hitler insisted that a dozen assault guns be completed monthly with the howitzer, later increased to two dozen. Aside from a pre-series batch, production began in February 1943.

## StuG III DEPLOYMENT

Assault-gun strength had increased from the four batteries available during the France campaign in 1940 to 11 battalions by the time of Operation *Barbarossa* in the summer of 1941. These battalions were allocated to the field armies. The new long-barreled StuG III began arriving in Russia by the spring of 1942, which considerably improved the ability of these units to defend against Soviet tank attack.

The antitank performance of the StuG III with the long L/48 gun was reinforced by the crews' excellent artillery training and better fire-control sights. A report by the Heer's Waffenamt in September 1943 reported that "the kill rates of assault gun batteries are frequently higher than those of Panzer units even though both are equipped with the same main gun." Indeed a report to Hitler in August 1943 after the Kursk battles indicated that "the reports from the front submitted to the Führer highlight the exceptional value of the assault gun which in several cases under the prevailing combat conditions proved superior to the Panzer IV." It is worth noting that in October 1943, Guderian authorized a special table of equipment for a Panzer StuG company to be used in Panzer units when there were shortages of Panther and Tiger tanks. By the end of 1943, only about half (54 percent) of the assault guns were in the assault-gun battalions. More than a quarter (25.3 percent) were assigned to Panzer divisions, 13 percent were assigned to the Waffen-SS and about 2 percent to Luftwaffe units. The Sturmartillerie had become so successful that in early 1944, the Heer considered making it possible to volunteer for assignment to the StuG battalions.

| StuG strength and losses, 1941–45 | | | | |
|---|---|---|---|---|
| Month | StuG strength | StuH 42 strength | StuG losses* | StuH 42 losses* |
| June 1941 | 377 | 0 | 4 | 0 |
| September 1941 | 479 | 0 | 42 | 0 |
| December 1941 | 598 | 0 | 49 | 0 |
| March 1942 | 625 | 0 | 88 | 0 |
| June 1942 | 697 | 0 | 51 | 0 |
| September 1942 | 873 | 0 | 89 | 0 |
| December 1942 | 1,039 | 0 | 102 | 0 |
| March 1943 | 1,111 | 5 | 410 | 8 |
| June 1943 | 1,216 | 109 | 93 | 0 |
| September 1943 | 1,716 | 146 | 489 | 29 |
| December 1943 | 1,877 | 100 | 574 | 34 |
| March 1944 | 2,415 | 182 | 756 | 51 |
| June 1944 | 2,804 | 272 | 632 | 46 |
| September 1944 | 2,655 | 412 | 1,628 | 198 |
| December 1944 | 3,105 | 539 | 539 | 162 |
| February 1945 | 3,607 | 577 | n/a | n/a |

*Cumulative quarterly total

The presence of StuG III provided a major boost to the morale of the German infantry during the increasingly difficult combat operations in 1943–44. It had been Manstein's intention since 1935 to assign assault guns directly to each infantry division. This practice was not possible until late in 1943 when StuG III production finally ramped up sufficiently. Under new organization structures, the Panzerjäger battalion attached to select infantry divisions had its first company equipped with

The StuG III first saw extensive service during the invasion of the Soviet Union in the summer of 1941. This is a StuG III Ausf B, armed with the initial L/24 short gun, of StuG-Abt 243 supporting the 71. Infanterie-Division. (NARA)

There was considerable detail change during the course of production of the StuG III Ausf G at Alkett. This particular example, knocked out during fighting against the 110th Infantry, 28th Division near Le Neubourg on August 24, 1944, has the late-style return rollers characteristic of Alkett vehicles starting in January 1944. It is fitted with the Saukopf mantlet introduced in October 1943 and the shot deflector in front of the commander's cupola introduced in September 1943. (NARA)

towed or self-propelled 7.5cm PaK 40 antitank guns, and the second company with assault guns. By the middle of 1944, the number of these companies had increased considerably with about 1,400 assault guns in service, and an aim to have about 4,000 in service by the spring of 1945 and 6,500 by the late summer of 1945. As will be detailed below, StuG III production was not sufficient for this ambitious objective, so these companies would in many cases be equipped with a new, low-cost assault gun based on the Czech PzKpfw 38(t) chassis.

From the start of Operation *Barbarossa* in June 1941 through August 1944, Sturmgeschütz units claimed 18,261 kills against Soviet AFVs; propaganda reports rounded this out to 20,000. Total German claims against Soviet AFVs during this period totaled 100,748, so the StuG claims represented nearly a fifth (18 percent), which is remarkable considering that this was not the AFV's primary mission. Nevertheless, tank fighting was only a small fraction of the missions of the Sturmartillerie. In August 1944, the head of the Panzer artillery branch reported to the Heer high command that

> A review of targets engaged by the assault artillery and ammunition expenditures confirms the firm opinion of the artillery command that the assault artillery does not fire primarily at tanks. When tanks do appear, the assault guns then aim exclusively at them. Since assault artillery is always employed at the focal point of the battle, tanks must always be part of the equation. Nevertheless, the majority of artillery targets are in the infantry's combat mission. In recent months, operations against enemy antitank forces and mortars have grown in intensity and significance.

From December 1, 1943 to May 31, 1944, 23 StuG III units on the Eastern Front fired a total of 315,280 rounds, of which 263,685 (83.7 percent) were fired against unarmored targets such as infantry, buildings, and vehicles, while 51,595 (16.3 percent) were fired against tanks and other armored targets. This resulted in claims for 1,899 Soviet AFVs destroyed as well as 132 disabled. Curiously enough, this suggests that it took more than 25 rounds of ammunition for every Soviet tank destroyed or disabled. During this period, 436 StuG III were lost in combat, for an exchange ratio of about 4-to-1.

The combat debut of the StuG was the May–June 1940 battle of France. However, Guderian's displeasure over the diversion of PzKpfw III production to the assault guns limited the initial force to a paltry four batteries in 1940. (NARA)

By the beginning of 1944, there were 38 StuG battalions deployed with nine more being organized and trained. Another change under way in 1944 was an effort to provide the assault-gun battalion with organic Panzergrenadier support in an escort battery (Begleit-Batterie) with ten SdKfz 251 half-tracks. There was also an effort to expand the assault-gun battalions in size from 31 assault guns (three batteries with ten vehicles each, plus one command vehicle) to 45 assault guns (three companies, each with 14 vehicles plus one command vehicle). In the event, only four of these enlarged units were deployed.

To add further to the confusing proliferation of StuG III units in 1944, the Heer decided on a cosmetic change in the unit designation. Instead of being designated as battalions (Sturmgeschütz-Abteilungen), the assault-gun units as of February 14, 1944 were to be renamed as brigades (Sturmgeschütz-Brigaden). This was purely a propaganda move, and there was no change in unit strength. Likewise the assault-gun companies in the divisional Panzerjäger-Abteilungen were redesignated as battalions. To muddy the waters yet more, in early October 1944 the divisional assault-gun battalions reverted back to the company designation.

Guderian had remained antagonistic towards the assault-gun concept and saw it as a rival to the Panzer force. He continued to insist that the divisional assault-gun companies focus their attention on the antitank mission and he encouraged the use of the term "Jäger" when referring to the StuG III in these units. When Guderian replaced Generaloberst Kurt Zeitzler as chief of the general staff in the late summer of 1944, the rapid growth of the assault-gun force came to an end. Under Guderian's direction, the number of assault-gun brigades was capped at 45. Due to the Normandy landings in June 1944 and the need to transfer units to the West, the number of assault-gun brigades on the Eastern Front inevitably shrank. Three or four assault-gun brigades were deployed to France in the summer of 1944, another four were deployed in Italy and the Balkans, and there were usually five to seven brigades refitting in Germany at any given time due to the catastrophic losses in the summer 1944 fighting. Besides the StuG brigades, there was an increasing use of StuG III in Panzer units as substitutes for tanks and tank destroyers.

Aside from their use in Sturmartillerie units, there was an increasing use of assault guns as tank substitutes in 1944 such as this StuG III Ausf G in 2./Pz-Abt 103, lost near Cori, Italy in May 1944. The smoke candles on the superstructure side were a feature of the vehicles manufactured between February and May 1943. (NARA)

## THE "ERSATZ STURMGESCHÜTZ"

The decision to expand significantly the number of divisional assault companies faced the obvious difficulty of the limited production resources available for the StuG III. The shortage of production capacity was exacerbated by the RAF raid on Berlin on November 26, 1943 that severely damaged Alkett, the main StuG plant. One option was to switch one of the Czech factories to StuG III production, but a December 1943 report to Hitler concluded that the BMM plant (the former Czechoslovak ČKD) did not have the capacity to produce such a large vehicle with thick armor plate. Instead, a proposal emerged for a 13,000kg (14.3-ton) "leichte Panzerjäger auf 38(t)." A wooden mockup was hastily prepared in January 1944, and Romanian histories claim that it was inspired by their own Mareşal tank destroyer that had been in development with Czech assistance since the summer of 1943.[3] Whatever the origins, the new design was approved for production and the first vehicle completed in March 1944. The plan was to convert both the BMM plant and Škoda plant to the production of 500 per month at each plant by March 1945, an astonishing objective by German standards. In the event, Guderian's growing influence with Hitler led to the decision officially to designate it as the leichte Jagdpanzer 38(t) rather than as a Sturmgeschütz. Nevertheless, its primary mission was to serve as a cheap substitute for the StuG III in divisional assault-gun companies. It was sometimes called the Hetzer, though this name is in fact a misnomer.[4]

---

3   For further details of Mareşal, see Steven J. Zaloga, *Tanks of Hitler's Eastern Allies 1941–45*, Osprey New Vanguard 199.

4   On the controversy of the Hetzer name, see Hilary Doyle & Tom Jentz, *Jagdpanzer 38 Hetzer*, Osprey New Vanguard 36.

The Jagdpanzer 38(t) was developed as an inexpensive substitute for the StuG III for use in divisional assault-gun companies. This vehicle of 2./PzJg-Abt 1708 of the 708. Volkgrenadier-Division was knocked out in Halloville, France on November 17, 1944 by an M10 of the 813th TD Battalion in support of the 79th Division. (NARA)

The other StuG III substitute was the StuG IV. In the wake of the November 1943 bombing of the Alkett plant, a decision was made in early December 1943 to create a direct substitute on the larger PzKpfw IV chassis. This was a straightforward adaptation, and the first StuG IV were completed later in December 1943 at the Krupp Grusonwerk. A total of 1,141 were completed by the end of the war. They were used in an identical fashion to the StuG III, but most were deployed with the StuG companies in various infantry divisions.

The StuG IV used a modified fighting compartment design from the StuG III except that there was an extension on the left front corner for the driver. This particular vehicle served with SS-Pz-Abt 17 of the 17. SS-Panzergrenadier-Division and was hit by Ninth Air Force fighter-bombers along the Marigny–Montreuil road in late July 1944 during the Operation *Cobra* breakout. (NARA)

# THE StuG III VS THE WESTERN ALLIES

The StuG III saw most of its combat employment on the Eastern Front, and even as late as December 1944 there were three times as many Sturmgeschütz brigades in the East. Aside from the handful of early StuG III in France in 1940, the next contact with the type in the West was in North Africa. Three StuG III Ausf C and D were part of Sonderverband zbV 288, which was sent to North Africa in 1942. Rommel requested that a full StuG battalion be sent to the Deutsches Afrikakorps to support his infantry units, and StuG-Abt 242 was raised for this purpose in November 1942. However, before it was sent to North Africa, two of its companies were sent to the Eastern Front. The remaining company, 1./StuG-Abt 242, finally deployed to Tunisia in early 1943 with four StuG III Ausf F/8 and was attached to the 10. Panzer-Division. It was renamed as Sturmgeschütz-Batterie 90 at the end of April 1943. The battery fought in the final campaigns in Tunisia, finally surrendering to British forces on Cape Bon in May 1943. Curiously enough, some veterans' photos from US M10 battalions show a knocked-out StuG III, so it is possible that the first contact between the StuG III and M10 occurred in North Africa. Sicily was the first campaign where the Allies encountered more than a handful of StuG III. The Panzer-Division "Hermann Göring" had about 20 StuG III, and these saw extensive combat use in the July–August 1943 fighting. StuG-Abt 247 was deployed on Sardinia in this time period due to German concerns that the Allies might stage an amphibious landing there; it was transferred to Corsica in September 1943 and never saw fighting against Allied forces in this theater.

The first encounters with StuG battalions took place in Italy later in 1943. StuG-Abt 242 arrived in Italy in the late spring of 1943 and served in the army reserve around Pisa. It was transferred to Sardinia and then Corsica in the fall of 1943, before returning to Italy in early 1944. The battalion had its batteries deployed to various hotspots, mainly on the Cassino front, where it saw extensive combat with Allied forces. It remained in Italy through the war, fighting the Allies in the Bologna area in 1945. The next Heer StuG battalion to arrive in Italy was StuG-Abt 907, which was committed to the counterattacks against the Anzio beachhead in January 1944. In March 1944, it was transferred to the Monte Cassino sector and spent the remainder of the war in Italy. The Luftwaffe also deployed its StuG-Abt 1 to the Anzio sector, but this unit was initially equipped with various types of Italian Semovente. The Heer's StuG-Abt 914 was deployed in Italy in February 1944, and was initially equipped with Italian Semovente M43 105/25 assault guns. The crews detested the obsolete Italian vehicles, and the unit was re-equipped with StuG III in September 1944, fighting in the late-fall battles in northern Italy around Modena. As of December 1944, these three brigades deployed a total of 93 StuG/StuH 42. The actual number of StuG III

The StuG III saw very little use in the North Africa battles. The first of these was a batch of three StuG III deployed with Sonderverband zbV 288 in 1942. This StuG III Ausf D has the special tropicalized engine deck fitted to these vehicles to assist in engine cooling. (MHI)

in the theater was higher, since there were some StuG III in Panzer divisions and other units. As of January 1945, there were 345 assault guns in German service in Italy, but this includes Italian Semovente. The last StuG unit to arrive in Italy was StuG-Abt 107 in early 1945.

## StuG III IN THE ETO

The Wehrmacht began reinforcing Heeresgruppe B (Army Group B) in France in the fall of 1943 in preparation for the anticipated Allied amphibious invasion. An assault-gun school was established at Tours to raise and train units in this theater. During the initial fighting in Normandy in June 1944, there were only two StuG brigades deployed in France, StuG-Brig 902, which was the Tours training unit converted into a combat unit, and the Luftwaffe's Fallschirmjäger StuG-Brig 911. However, there were numerous StuG III present in other formations, including three Panzer-Kompanien (Funklenk) – companies armed with radio-controlled demolition tanks – and four infantry divisions (243., 346., 352., and 353.) with a company of StuG III in their organic Panzerjäger units. Several Waffen-SS Panzer divisions had StuG III in place of other AFVs; for example, the 1. and 2. SS-Panzer-Divisionen each had 45 StuG III as substitutes in their Panzerjäger units while the 9. and 10. SS-Panzer-Divisionen each had a company of 40 StuG III to make up for a shortage of tanks. Besides the StuG III, the 17. SS-Panzergrenadier-Division had 42 StuG IV. As of June 10, 1944, there were 158 assault guns in Panzer units in the West, plus a similar amount in the StuG brigades and assorted companies. StuG strength in France continued to increase, with two more StuG brigades committed to the fighting, StuG-Brig 341 at the end of July and StuG-Brig 394 in early August. A total of more than 450 assault guns were deployed on the Normandy front during the summer fighting in both Panzer and Sturmgeschütz formations.

The first Allied contact with the StuG III in Normandy occurred on D-Day when a platoon from StuG-Abt 1243, the divisional assault-gun company of the 243. Infanterie-Division, supported the counterattack by Gren-Rgt 1058 against the 82nd Airborne Division positions on the north side of Sainte-Mère-Église. Two of the StuG III Ausf G were knocked out by 57mm antitank guns of the 80th Airborne Antiaircraft Battalion. (NARA)

# M10

## ORIGINS

The stunning defeat of France in June 1940 caused considerable alarm in the US Army. This came at a critical time, since the US Army was in transition from its emaciated peacetime state to an expanded wartime footing. Senior commanders grappled with the dilemma of what types of weapons and tactics would be needed to deal with German Blitzkrieg attacks as seen in France in 1940. Senior cavalry officers such as Major General Adna Chaffee, Jr saw American tank divisions as the best antidote to Blitzkrieg, and the Armored Force was established at Fort Knox, Kentucky on July 10, 1940. However, influential artillery officers were convinced that other approaches were needed to defend infantry divisions. By far the most influential officer in this debate was Lieutenant General Lesley McNair, who led the Army Ground Forces (AGF) headquarters until his death in 1944. In May 1941, the Army chief-of-staff, General George C. Marshall, ordered that an offensive antitank force be created. After some expedient solutions such as antitank battalions were tested in war games, in December 1941 McNair established the Tank Destroyer Center at Fort Hood, Texas to promote new alternatives. Led by Major General Andrew Bruce, the Tank Destroyer Center continued to experiment with different tactical approaches to the Blitzkrieg threat.

The outcome of these studies was a set of tactics epitomized by the Tank Destroyer motto "Seek, Strike, Destroy." Instead of relying on a linear barrier of towed antitank guns, the Center proposed the creation of a new type of tank-destroyer battalion based on mobile antitank guns. These battalions would be concentrated at corps levels, and when a Panzer division ruptured a defensive line, they would rush forward en masse

The original conception of the T35 was a simple shield for the 3in gun with no protection overhead or to the rear. This is the original wooden mock-up of the design. (NARA)

19.6ft

and crush the breakthrough with concentrated antitank firepower. While there was a general consensus on the new tactics, the question of the ideal tank destroyer proved more difficult to solve. By the time that the Tank Destroyer Center had emerged, the United States had already been dragged into war in both Europe and the Pacific. There were enormous demands on industry to meet the exorbitant demands of the new armored divisions as well as British orders for American tanks and other AFVs. With the new tank-destroyer battalions already being organized, equipment was needed immediately, even if not an ideal design.

An expedient light tank destroyer was created by mounting the 37mm antitank gun in the rear of a ¾-ton truck as the M6 37mm GMC, and an expedient heavy tank destroyer was similarly slapped together by mounting the French 75mm M1897 gun in an M3 half-track as the M3 75mm GMC. Major General Bruce was frustrated with both designs, as the M6 37mm GMC had poor cross-country performance, poor protection, and its gun traverse was limited to the rear. The M3 75mm GMC also suffered from very limited traverse and Bruce felt that its cross-country speed was inadequate. In spite of their limitations, these types formed the basis for the first tank-destroyer battalions and were the first tank destroyers to see combat in Tunisia in early 1943. As Bruce feared, their performance was lackluster, the M6 37mm GMC being particularly poor.

From the outset, the Tank Destroyer Command wanted a fully tracked design with a more powerful gun. Bruce described the ideal tank destroyer as "a cruiser not a battleship," with the accent on speed rather than armored protection. So the tank destroyer would have less armor than contemporary tanks, but greater speed and more firepower. The first Ordnance full-track designs such as the M5 3in GMC on a Cletrac tractor and the M9 3in GMC on an M3 medium-tank chassis were hasty expedients

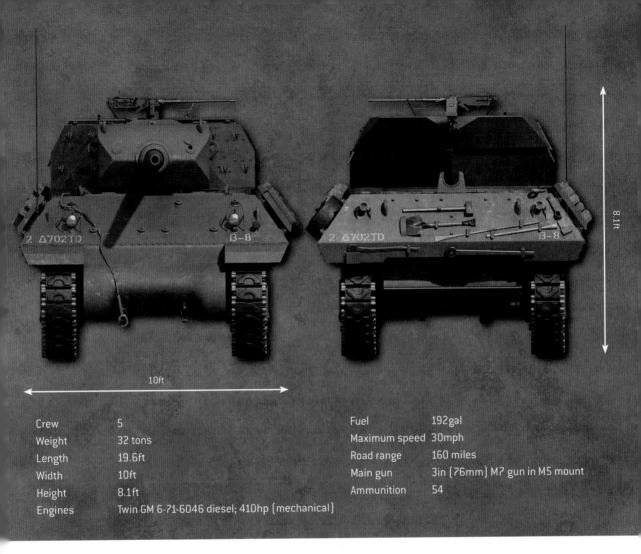

| | | | | |
|---|---|---|---|---|
| Crew | 5 | | Fuel | 192gal |
| Weight | 32 tons | | Maximum speed | 30mph |
| Length | 19.6ft | | Road range | 160 miles |
| Width | 10ft | | Main gun | 3in (76mm) M7 gun in M5 mount |
| Height | 8.1ft | | Ammunition | 54 |
| Engines | Twin GM 6-71-6046 diesel; 410hp (mechanical) | | | |

and were not accepted for production. In November 1941, Ordnance proposed the creation of a turreted tank destroyer combining the 3in gun in use on the M6 heavy tank with the M4A2 medium-tank chassis. The original design of the new tank destroyer put the gun in a partial turret that only offered frontal protection. This was reflective of the influence of artillery officers, who saw the weapon as a mechanized antitank gun that only needed enough frontal armor to protect the gun crew against shrapnel. It was never envisioned that the tank destroyer would slug it out with enemy tanks. As detail design proceeded beyond the first wooden mock-up, the new T35 3in GMC was fitted with an open-top turret, but with protection all around. The protective armor was sufficient to shield the crew from machine-gun fire, but not adequate to defend it against antitank guns except in the front quadrant.

Reports from tank fighting in the Philippines in December 1941 and January 1942 complained about the vulnerability of horizontal armor, and prompted the redesign of the T35 hull with sloped sides for better protection. This resulted in the heavily modified T35E1 pilot. The T35 and T35E1 pilots were delivered from General Motors' Fisher Body Division to the Aberdeen Proving Ground in Maryland in April 1942. Trials favored the T35E1, but Ordnance feared that the original cast turret would be too difficult to manufacture and quickly asked Fisher to develop a welded alternative.

The T35 pilot used a cast turret on an M4A2 tank hull as seen here. The hull was subsequently redesigned in the T35E1, which became the pattern for the standard M10 tank destroyer. (NARA)

In addition, the T35E1 pilot weighed over 30 tons and so the armor was reduced from 1in (25.4mm) to 0.75in (19.1mm). Mounting bosses were fitted to the exterior so that additional appliqué armor could be attached if deemed necessary; in the event, no appliqué armor kits were ever produced, so this feature became useless. Bruce opposed the T35E1 design, arguing that it did not offer a sufficient advancement in speed and mobility over the M4 Sherman medium tank. He was overruled by Lieutenant General McNair, who felt that an adequate tank destroyer available now was preferable to an ideal tank destroyer that would not be available for more than a year.

The modified T35E1 design was accepted for Army service in June 1942 as the M10 3in GMC. The Army was so desperate for an adequate tank destroyer that M10 production was given an AA1 industrial priority rating, higher even than the new M4 Sherman tank. Production began in September 1942, and the related M10A1 with the engine from the M4A3 medium tank was also accepted for service. The first units were equipped with the M10 and M10A1 in December 1942. For the sake of standardization, the US Army decided to field only the diesel-powered M10 into combat zones, while the gasoline-powered M10A1 was retained for stateside training. The M10 design did not undergo major changes except for one serious issue, the turret counterweight problem. The original turret lacked any counterweights at the rear of the turret. It became quickly evident that the heavy barrel led to such a severe weight imbalance that the turret was difficult to traverse, especially when on a slope. A "quick-fix" solution was first used in late 1942 by placing simple counterweights on the upper rear turret plates. A more elaborate wedge-shaped counterweight was adopted in January 1943. Although an adequate solution, it added 3,700lb to the vehicle. The fourth and final approach, dubbed the duck-bill counterweight, was developed in March 1943. This required a redesign of the turret rear, but reduced the counterweight to only 2,500lb. In total, 4,993 M10 were manufactured from September 1942 to December 1943, while a further 1,413 M10A1 were completed from October 1942 to November 1943 for a grand total of 6,406 vehicles.

## M10 COMBAT DEPLOYMENT

The first tank-destroyer (TD) battalions went into combat in Tunisia in early 1943. Neither the M6 37mm GMC nor the M3 75mm GMC were effective designs, and their problems were compounded by the novelty of their tactics. Commanders were unwilling to leave vehicles in reserve until the appearance of German tanks, and so the tank destroyers were often deployed forward to provide fire support regardless of their doctrine. Tank-destroyer tactical doctrine was widely ignored, and instead of massing the tank destroyers, higher commands often broke up the battalions into constituent companies and sent them off on separate support missions. The M6 37mm GMC proved so poor in combat that it was hastily withdrawn from service as a hazard to its crews. In their first serious combat test, the tank-destroyer battalions failed at Kasserine Pass and one of the battalions was wiped out in the process.

The M3 75mm GMC proved useful in some circumstances. The 601st TD Battalion put up a spirited defense against the 10. Panzer-Division during the battle of El Guettar on March 23, 1943, though at a cost of 27 of its 36 tank destroyers. The combat debut of the M10 3in GMC occurred after the Kasserine Pass fighting with the deployment of the 776th and 899th TD battalions to Tunisia. The 899th TD Battalion was the first to see combat, fighting in the battle of El Guettar and losing seven M10s in the process. The two battalions saw very little antitank fighting for the remainder of the Tunisian campaign, because by this stage of the war the Panzer force had been substantially reduced. The commander of the idle 776th TD Battalion convinced corps commanders that the battalion could be usefully used to deepen the corps artillery, since the tank-destroyer crewmen had been trained in standard field-artillery indirect-fire techniques. The battalion was successfully used in this fashion for the remainder of the campaign, foreshadowing a frequent role for the M10 in the subsequent Italian campaign.

The tank-destroyer force had proven to be a major disappointment in the Tunisian campaign, so much so that no tank destroyers were deployed during Operation *Husky*,

This is the pilot for the M10A1, which was powered by the Ford GAA engine as used on the M4A3 medium tank. An early attempt to correct the turret imbalance was to stow grousers on the upper rear turret panel as seen here, but this was a completely inadequate solution. (NARA)

The M10 saw its combat debut in Tunisia in March 1943 with two tank-destroyer battalions. This vehicle, named "Invincible," is from the early-production series with the first style of "quick-fix" turret counterweights and was photographed at Oran in March 1943. (NARA)

the invasion of Sicily in July 1943. A fact-finding tour by Lieutenant General Jacob Devers, head of the Armored Force, concluded that the tank-destroyer concept was a failure and that the best opponent of the Panzer was a tank and not a tank destroyer. Other officers were less critical and felt that training and preparation had been inadequate. In the event, the high hopes of the Tank Destroyer Center were dashed and the original 1941 plans for 220 tank-destroyer battalions were trimmed back to 144, and later in the year to only 106. Of these, 61 were eventually sent to Italy or Europe and ten to the Pacific; the remaining 35 were disbanded before seeing combat.

The problem with the US tank-destroyer doctrine was that it was based on the unique circumstances of the 1940 France campaign, and attempted to develop technology and tactics that would have succeeded where the French Army had failed. The two key flaws in this requirement were that the US Army would seldom be on the operational defensive against the Wehrmacht in World War II, and that German tactics were changing. Bruce continued to focus on the tactical notion that a very mobile tank-destroyer force would prove valuable in defending against massed Panzer attack. In the absence of massed Panzer attack, the doctrine had little value and Bruce's focus on mobility was a serious distraction. Bruce might have steered the focus of the Tank Destroyer Center towards the more pertinent aim of ensuring that the tank destroyers evolved in firepower to overmatch advances in German armored protection. Instead, Bruce remained complacent about the need for more potent antitank guns, and the advances that were made in this direction such as the 90mm gun were undertaken by Ordnance in spite of Bruce's inattention. By the summer of 1944, the tank destroyers were inadequate when facing newer German tanks such as the Panther.

McNair contributed to this problem both due to his parochial favoritism with respect to towed antitank weapons as well as a profoundly flawed procurement policy. McNair's AGF insisted that weapons would not be standardized unless they proved to have "battle-worthiness" and "battle-need." The "battle-worthiness" criterion was a reaction against the poor quality of US-manufactured weapons in World War I, and basically meant that AGF wanted all new weapons to be durable enough to be used overseas with a minimum of maintenance demands. His "battle-need" criterion was more insidious since it seemed so unobjectionable. McNair insisted that weapons would not be acquired unless there was a proven "battle-need", that is unless the troops in the field expressed a need for new weapons. The problem with this doctrine was that troops in the field did not have the time or the expertise to assess future weapons needs. Antitank technology was changing very rapidly between 1942 and 1944, and commanders in the field were not well briefed on new technological possibilities, nor were they well informed about the likely directions of German weapons development. By the time that troops in the field realized that a new weapon was needed, it was too late. It would take months or years before it was developed, entered production, and was shipped to the combat theater. On top of that, troops had to be trained to use weaponry, and in the case of a new antitank gun, a new family of ammunition also had to be prepared and delivered. What was needed was a predictive policy that anticipated future weapons needs based on technical intelligence, and not McNair's reactive "battle-need" policy. This was not evident in 1943, when most US Army AFVs were as good or better than their German counterparts, but it became painfully clear in the ETO in 1944 when facing the new generation of German AFVs such as the Panther tank.

The firepower shortcomings of the M10's 3in gun in dealing with newer German AFVs such as the Panther led to the decision to begin replacing it as soon as possible with the M36 90mm GMC. The first M36 began arriving in the ETO during the fall of 1944; this shows a comparison of the M10 (to the left) and the M36 (to the right), both belonging to the 703rd TD Battalion, on October 24, 1944. (NARA)

The relative lack of Panzer opponents in Italy led to the growing use of the M10 tank destroyers in a secondary field-artillery role. This is an M10 of Company A, 804th TD Battalion near Coiano on October 7, 1944; the ground around it is littered with brass shell casings and fiber-board ammunition-transport tubes. (NARA)

Bruce hoped that the tank-destroyer doctrine would be validated by a faster tank destroyer more suited to the flawed tactical doctrine, and he placed his hopes on the new M18 76mm GMC. This was the fastest AFV in US Army service in World War II, with a road speed of up to 55mph. It saw its combat debut at Anzio in early 1944, where its high speed did not prove to be especially useful while its thin armor and cramped interior led tank-destroyer crews to dismiss it as inferior to the M10. While Bruce was pushing for the M18, McNair used the Tunisian failure as an excuse to revert back to a towed antitank gun versus a self-propelled weapon. He ordered the production of a towed version of the 3in gun and the conversion of a portion of the tank-destroyer force from the M10 to the towed 3in gun. By D-Day in June 1944, 11 of the 30 tank-destroyer battalions in the ETO were in the towed configuration. These towed battalions proved to be ineffective in combat and were gradually converted back to self-propelled configuration later in 1944.

Tank-destroyer battalions proved to be increasingly marginal in the Italian campaign. They were ineffective in repulsing the Panzer counterattacks against the Allied beachhead at Salerno in September 1943 due to their small numbers, and were not much more useful at the Anzio beachhead in January and February 1944 for the same reason. They were seldom used in the antitank role in the fighting along the Volturno River in the fall of 1943 or in the Monte Cassino fighting, since there were few attacking Panzers. As often as not, they were used in the expedient role of field artillery to enhance corps or division artillery in indirect-fire missions.

In spite of the irrelevance of their antitank role in the Italian fighting, the tank-destroyer battalions proved valuable during the reformation of US Army tactical doctrine in the wake of the Kasserine Pass debacle. The US Army had

A M10 3in GMC of Company B, 803rd TD Battalion named "Bouncing TNT," seen in England in April 1944 prior to D-Day. This is from the final production version with the enlarged turret and duck-bill counterweights. (NARA)

parroted Guderian's massed Panzerkorps approach in the organization of its own Armored Force, to the detriment of the traditional tank role of infantry support. While there was no denying the importance of armored divisions in offensive operations, at the same time the infantry still required armored support to carry out its mission. The small number of separate tank battalions available in Tunisia was used on an expedient basis for infantry support and was found to be extremely valuable in this role. Infantry commanders argued that each division should have a battalion or more of tanks for the close-support mission. McNair continued to oppose the incorporation of AFVs into infantry divisions, but the tide was now shifting in favor of this approach. The reorganization of the US armored divisions in the wake of the Tunisian campaign in 1943 freed up many tank battalions, and by early 1944 there was a general consensus that each infantry division should have the support of a tank battalion during offensive operations.

The Italian campaign completely undermined any remaining support for the tank-destroyer battalion's antitank focus, but it did highlight the potential use of the battalion for infantry support. It could be used much like a tank for direct-fire support, and in other circumstances it could be profitably used by divisional artillery to deepen its own indirect-fire mission. Rather than simply disband all of the tank-destroyer battalions, those already deployed in Italy and the ETO gradually saw their mission shift to the infantry-support role to reinforce the separate tank battalions. By the time of the Normandy landings in June 1944, the US Army was moving to an expedient tactic of reinforcing each infantry division on offensive operations with a tank battalion and a tank-destroyer battalion. This became the standard operating procedure in the 1944–45 ETO campaigns.

# TECHNICAL SPECIFICATIONS

## FIREPOWER

Both the M10 3in GMC and the StuG III Ausf G had guns capable of penetrating each other at typical combat ranges. Overall, the M10 had superior firepower due to the use of a traversable turret, which made it more effective in a wider range of tactical circumstances. Several types of antitank ammunition were available for both types of vehicles, and the accompanying chart lists the common type in use in the fall of 1944. Enhanced antitank ammunition was not common in the fall 1944 fighting. The tungsten-core PzGr 40 was not widely available to StuG III units in the West in 1944, while the new American tungsten-core M93 HVAP did not become widespread until later in the year. The high-explosive round of the StuG III had a larger high-explosive fill than that on the M10's 3in gun, but growing problems with high-explosive quality in German production in 1944 reduced some of this advantage.

The StuG III offered excellent antitank accuracy due to better sighting equipment than comparable Panzers. The vehicle commander operated a Scherenfahrlafetten SF 14Z scissors telescope offering 10× magnification, which was superior in resolution to the binoculars available to Panzer commanders. The Selbstfahrlafetten Zielfernrohr Sfl ZF 1a gunner's sight on the StuG III provided 5× magnification, while that on most Panzers was 2.5×. There was considerable controversy in the Wehrmacht over the

relative advantages of artillery-style fire controls as well as artillery crew training for the StuG III crew. The StuG III crews traditionally used the artillery style of "bracketing," firing a first round high, and then adjusting lower until the target was struck; Panzer crews were taught to "walk their fire" to the target. In comparative tests, the artillery style was found to be quicker and more economical.

| Gun technical comparison | | |
|---|---|---|
| | StuG III Ausf G | M10 3in GMC |
| Main gun | StuK 40 | M7 |
| Caliber | 7.5cm | 3in (76mm) |
| Tube length | L/48 | L/50 |
| Armor-piercing projectile | PzGr 39 | M62A1 |
| Type | APCBC | APC |
| Penetration (mm; @500m (547yd), 30 degrees) | 96 | 92 |
| High-explosive projectile | SprGr 34 | M42A1 |
| Projectile weight | 5.7kg (12lb 9.1oz) | 12lb 13.6oz |
| Explosive fill | 650g (22.9oz) | 13.8oz |

The late-production StuG III Aus G had a number of distinctive features including the Saukopf cast mantlet, the coaxial machine evident from the firing port in the mantlet, and the remote-controlled machine-gun station on the roof. This particular vehicle was lost during the fighting in the Ardennes in December 1944. (MHI)

The M10 3in GMC was provided with both tank-style direct-fire instruments as well as artillery sights. The M10 used the M51 or the improved M70G 3× direct-sighting telescope for direct fire. It was also fitted with an M1 gunner's quadrant and M12 panoramic artillery telescope for indirect-fire artillery missions. While the M10 was regularly used for indirect-fire missions, the Wehrmacht actively discouraged the use of the StuG III in this role for fear of excessive barrel wear.

The most significant difference in firepower between the two types was in weapons traverse, with the M10 having an advantage in close combat due to its turret. The StuG III gun was limited to a traverse of 10 degrees to either side of the centerline. This was not a critical disadvantage if the StuG III was in an overwatch or ambush position at long range from its target, but it became a significant tactical risk at closer ranges or in fine-grain terrain. Generaloberst Guderian, long a critic of the Sturmgeschütz concept, pointed out these shortcomings to Hitler in a report in late June 1944 based on recent Normandy experiences:

> Combat lessons from Sicily, Italy and Normandy comparing the PzKpfw IV to the Sturmgeschütz unanimously state that when employed on coastal roads, mountainous terrain, and in the sunken lanes and hedges of Normandy, the Sturmgeschütz is both tactically and technically considerably less favored that the PzKpfw IV. Terrain makes aiming impossible or at least limits the Sturmgeschütz towards the sides ... Employment of the Sturmgeschütz in the sunken lanes and hedges of Normandy is difficult because the gun is mounted too low. In contrast, the PzKpfw IV can fire out of the sunken lanes and over hedge because of the height of the gun and the traversing turret.

While Guderian's points were technically correct, it is worth pointing out that many German infantry commanders preferred the StuG III in other terrain conditions specifically because its low silhouette made it less visible, and hence less vulnerable to enemy fire.

## ZF1A TELESCOPIC GUN SIGHT, 7.5cm StuK 40, StuG III

The StuG III's Selbstfahrlafetten Zielfernrohr Sfl ZF 1a gunner's sight offered 5× magnification. The Sfl ZF 1a telescopic sight had an engraved reticle consisting of an aiming triangle in the center with smaller triangles on either side. The gunner placed the target at the apex of the center triangle. This reticle provided a limited stadiametric ranging capability, which allowed a well-trained gunner to estimate the range based on the size of the target compared to the large triangle. The unit of measure was a graduation (*strich*) equaling 1m at 1,000m range, with the larger triangle having sides of four graduations and the smaller triangle having sides of two graduations. So for example, an M10 was about 3m (10ft) wide, so if the front view of the vehicle filled the center triangle, it was about 750m (820yd) away. Needless to say, such calculations were too difficult in the heat of battle, so a gunner had to be so well trained that the procedure became instinctive. The series of triangles was intended to provide the gunner with a method to gauge the speed of a crossing target, but once again, this was too complicated to calculate during real engagements and depended on excellent training. In this case, the M10 is seen at point-blank range, and so no adjustments were needed.

Neither the StuG III nor M10 were ideal infantry-support platforms due to poor machine-gun armament. On many occasions, machine guns were invaluable for attacking enemy infantry at close ranges, and they were widely used in this fashion by both German and American tanks. Tanks typically had at least two machine guns, usually a bow-mounted hull machine gun and a coaxial machine gun in the turret. In some cases they had a third machine gun on the turret roof for antiaircraft defense. Both the StuG III and M10 had a machine gun, but the configuration was far from ideal for use in infantry support.

On the standard versions of the StuG III Ausf G, an MG 34 or MG 42 machine gun was carried for self-defense; it was mounted behind a shield over the loader's hatch. While the shield provided a modest amount of frontal protection to the loader when firing the weapon, he was still highly exposed from the side and rear. In response to severe criticisms of the shortcomings of this mounting from the Eastern Front, a remote-controlled weapons mount (*Rundumsfeuer*) was developed that permitted the firing of the machine gun from within the protective armor of the vehicle. This began to appear sporadically on assault guns built by Alkett in July 1944, but did not become standard in production until October 1944. A scheme to fit a coaxial machine gun through an opening in the gun mantlet began to appear on assault guns built at MIAG in May 1944, and on Alkett production vehicles between June and August 1944.

The M10 mounted a .50-caliber heavy machine gun on a pintle mount at the rear of the turret for antiaircraft defense. This location was very poorly suited to the use of the weapon against enemy infantry and other ground targets, since a crewman had to exit the turret and fire the machine gun while standing exposed on the rear engine deck. In addition, this caused significant problems inside the turret due to the muzzle blast. Since the M10 was already out of production by the summer of 1944, there were no factory fixes for the issue. Instead, there were sporadic efforts by units in the field to move the machine gun from the turret rear to a front location by welding a pintle mount on one of the forward corners, most often on the left.

## M70G TELESCOPIC GUN SIGHT, 3in M7 GUN, M10 GMC

The M10 3in GMC used the M70G 3× direct-sighting telescope for direct fire. The M70G telescopic sight had a small switch that enabled the reticle to be illuminated in poor lighting conditions. The reticle had range gradations for the standard 3in M62A1 APC armor-piercing projectile; the performance of the HE projectile was essentially similar at ranges under 1,000yd. The reticle pattern was graduated in yards, so the commander estimated the range to target using his binoculars, included this in his firing commands, and the gunner adjusted the sight on the target accordingly.

The StuG III Ausf F introduced the longer L/48 gun. This is an assault gun of 2./StuG-Abt 210 in the port of Novorossiysk after its capture in early September 1942 during the fighting in the Kuban. The battalion was nicknamed "Tigerkopf" for its tiger-head insignia. (NARA)

# COMMAND AND CONTROL

Both the StuG III Ausf G and the M10 3in GMC were fitted with radios for communication among the vehicles within sub-units as well as to provide connections with higher headquarters. In general, the M10 3in GMC had communication advantages in the 1944–45 period, due to its use of FM radios and the greater availability of additional AFV–infantry radios to enhance cooperation with neighboring infantry units. German radio practices atrophied in 1944–45 due to the poverty of radio resources in the Heer in the final year of the war.

The standard radio fit in the StuG III was the FuG 16, which was a 10-watt short-wave transceiver that operated in the 27.2–33.3MHz bands. The StuG III of platoon and higher commanders had the expanded FuG 15 set, which added an additional receiver to monitor a broader range of communication networks. StuG IIIs that were part of Panzer units had a different radio fit (FuG 2 and FuG 5), which operated in different bands. German radios were of good quality, but AM radios had inherent limits when used from moving AFVs. The StuG III radios did not operate on the same bands as German small-unit infantry radios, and due to a shortage of electronic resources it was seldom possible to equip StuG III units with additional radios for direct links to the infantry subunits they were supporting. Instead, the StuG III used traditional methods, either using the existing radio network to communicate with the infantry battalion or the regimental radio network that then indirectly contacted the infantry subunits, or relied on more traditional forms of signaling, including flares and hand-signals.

The M10 3in GMC was fitted with the SCR-610, which was an FM radio-transceiver operating in the 27.0–38.9MHz bands. The US Army rejected the use of AM radios for vehicle communication in 1941 due to the signal noise problem and standardized on FM radios much earlier than European armies. Aside from having better radio equipment, the US Army had a more generous supply of sets. One of the main tactical problems in AFV units supporting the infantry was the need to ensure rapid communication between both arms. As in the Wehrmacht, the US Army's AFV radios operated in different bands than the radios in infantry subunits. In 1944, US infantry companies had a SCR-300 "walkie-talkie" back-pack FM radio operating while the platoons had SCR-536 "handie-talkie" hand-held AM radios. As the problems of armor–infantry communication became evident in the 1944 Normandy fighting, the short-term solution was to supply the supporting tank-destroyer units with infantry radios. The common practice was to provide the tank-destroyer platoon leader with an SCR-300 radio to communicate with the infantry company leader. By the fall of 1944, a dedicated tank–infantry vehicular radio, the AN/VRC-3, was distributed, which was derived from the SCR-300.

The turret crew on the M10 consisted of three crewmen, shown here on an air-defense training exercise with the 811th TD Battalion at Camp Carson, Colorado in May 1943. The commander was stationed on the right side of the turret and is seen here observing with binoculars. The loader was also responsible for the .50-caliber heavy machine gun at the rear of the turret, while the gunner sat on the left side of the gun. (NARA)

# PROTECTION

Overall, the StuG III offered better armored protection than the M10. The M10 suffered from the open-turret configuration, which made it vulnerable to mortars and artillery as well as overhead small-arms fire. One of the immediate tactical consequences of this feature was the unsuitability of the M10 tank destroyers to be forward-deployed in defensive positions due to their vulnerability to German mortar fire. Tank-destroyer battalions discouraged the use of M10s in static positions near the front lines, though these warnings were often ignored by local infantry commanders. By the fall of 1944, a number of tank-destroyer battalions began to create improvised roof armor for their vehicles. Besides the open-roof issue, the M10 had thinner armor on most exposed surfaces than the StuG III. Some units adopted sandbags and other forms of appliqué armor in 1944 and 1945.

The StuG III Ausf G underwent continual armor upgrades during its manufacture to address the increasing lethality of Soviet antitank weapons. Alkett began adding an additional 30mm plate to the existing 50mm armor on the front superstructure and bow in the summer of 1942 and the initial production version of the StuG III Ausf G had this affixed with bolts or by welding. Between April and July 1943, the bolted appliqué on the bow was being replaced by integral 80mm armor plate, and the appliqué armor on the superstructure front used this method by the summer of 1944. In October 1943, Alkett introduced a cast-steel mantlet for the gun instead of the plate-armor type previously in use; some of the older type continued to appear in the production run due to shortages of the new type. Another type of protection upgrade seen in the final years of the war was the addition of concrete over the front corners of the vehicle.

37

The open roof of the M10 proved to be a significant tactical hazard in close combat. Some units developed roof-armor kits, and this is an example on a late-production M10 with the enlarged turret and duck-bill counterweights prepared by the 536th Ordnance Heavy Maintenance Company for units of the Seventh US Army in Lorraine in February 1945. (NARA)

| Comparative armor data | | | | |
|---|---|---|---|---|
| | StuG III Ausf G | | M10 3in GMC | |
| | Armor thickness (mm) | Slope (degrees) | Armor thickness (mm) | Slope (degrees) |
| Gun shield | 50 | 0 | 57 | 45 |
| Turret/ casemate side | 30 | 11 | 25 | 15 |
| Glacis | 30 | 86 | 38 | 55 |
| Bow | 80 | 20 | 51 | rounded |
| Upper hull side | 30 | 11 | 19 | 38 |
| Upper hull rear | 50 | 12 | 19 | 38 |
| Lower hull rear | 50 | 10 | 25 | 10 |

The initial up-armoring of the StuG III Ausf F/8 began at Alkett in September 1942 and the 30mm appliqué armor plates were welded to the bow and front of the superstructure as seen in the case of this vehicle, tactical number 001 of PzJg-Abt 61, 11. Panzer-Division, lost near Baume-les-Dames during the retreat from southern France in late August 1944. (MHI)

# THE COMBATANTS

## StuG III

### CREW

The StuG III Ausf G had a crew of four: the gun commander (Geschützführer), gunner (Richtkanonier), loader/radio operator (Ladekanonier/Funker), and driver (Fahrer). All of the crew was located on the left side of the vehicle except for the loader, who stood on the right side of the gun. The crew was all connected together through a vehicle intercom system via radio headsets and a throat mike. The gun commander was usually a non-commissioned officer and directed the crew from the left rear corner of the fighting compartment. On the StuG III Ausf G, the commander had a cupola fitted with eight periscopes for all-round vision. His main vision instrument was a scissors binocular, which was deployed through a small flap in the hatch for better armored protection. The commander was responsible for surveying the terrain for targets, and then instructing the driver roughly to aim the vehicle towards the objective, informing the gunner of the precise target and range, and the loader the type of ammunition. The gunner sat immediately in front of the commander and sighted through a periscopic telescope. The gun's elevation and traverse controls were manual. In front of the gunner in the front left side of the fighting compartment was the driver, whose vision was restricted to a single armored-glass episcope. The loader stood on the right side of the gun where most of the vehicle ammunition was located. The gunner was also cross-trained in radio operation and the radio was located in the sponson over

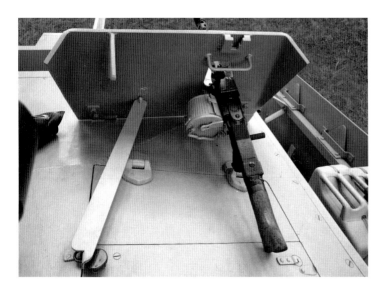

the right track. In addition, the loader manned the vehicle machine gun, which was located over his station. Although the StuG III had ammunition racks for 54 rounds, it was common for experienced crews to stow large amounts of additional ammunition inside the vehicle and on the engine deck, sometimes totaling a hundred rounds or more.

## GERMAN ASSAULT-GUN BRIGADES

The standard production StuG III Ausf G was fitted with an MG 42 machine gun behind an armored shield over the loader's hatch as seen here. Late-production versions had a remote-controlled machine-gun mount. [Author]

The standard Sturmgeschütz brigade – based on Kriegsstärkenachweisung Nr. 446 of June 1, 1944 – included 31 assault guns organized into three batteries plus a headquarters (Stab). Each Sturmgeschütz-Batterie included four sections: headquarters (Gruppe-Führer), which included the battery commander's StuG III; the combat battery (Gefechts-Batterie) with nine assault guns; the ammunition section (Munitionsstaffel); and the maintenance section (Kraftfahrzeug-Instandsetzgruppe). The combat battery was organized into three platoons (Züge) of three assault guns each. On paper, the 1. and 2. Züge were equipped with StuG III, while the 3. Zug was equipped with StuH 42. In practice, the organization depended on whatever types of assault guns were available.

By 1944, the Sturmgeschütz-Brigaden were usually subordinate to corps and were generally directed by the corps' artillery staff (Arko). Assault-gun doctrine favored the concentration of the brigade for decisive action, but with so little Panzer support available in the fall of 1944, the Sturmgeschütz brigades were usually dispersed to its infantry divisions, or even broken up into individual batteries and spread around to various hot spots. Ideally, an entire Sturmgeschütz-Brigade would be allotted to the infantry division that was at the focal point of an attack or counterattack. In such a case, the entire brigade could be used to support the regiment at the focus of the mission, or alternatively each of the division's three regiments would receive a battery in support. In turn, each regiment could allocate a single Sturmgeschütz platoon to each of its three battalions. In the event that only a single battery was allotted to a division, ideally the battery operated intact in support of the main objective; in practice a single platoon could be attached to each of the three infantry regiments. German tactical doctrine unequivocally rejected the use of single assault guns; the smallest acceptable tactical unit was the Zug of three assault guns.

In defensive combat, the Sturmgeschütz-Brigade was used primarily to respond to major penetrations of the main line of resistance (*Hauptkampflinie*), especially when it involved enemy tank attacks. German tactical doctrine stressed the need to respond to any enemy penetration with an immediate and forceful counterattack, and the Sturmgeschütz-Brigade was a powerful tool for any such mission. German tactical doctrine recognized the limitations of the Sturmgeschütz's limited traverse, and so the usual tactic was to employ the assault guns from overwatch positions behind the advancing infantry when facing a strong enemy defense. Even as late as 1944, the StuG III's gun was effective from a range of 2,000m (2,187yd), and tactical manuals discouraged the use of the assault guns at close ranges since it increased their vulnerability to fire against their weak flanks. Unlike tanks, the StuG III did not have an effective assortment of machine guns for offensive use against enemy infantry, so there was no reason for the vehicle to approach the enemy defense line too closely.

The left side of the StuG III interior was extremely cramped, as can be seen here with the commander peering through his SF 14Z scissors telescope and the gunner immediately in front of him. Out of sight is the driver, located further in front and below the gunner. (NARA)

One of the primary tactical problems in combined-arms tactics in World War II was the integration of armored and infantry forces. Ideally, German infantry divisions received tank–infantry training before combat, but by the fall of 1944 such training had become a luxury available to very few

units. Unlike the US Army, few German infantry divisions in 1944 had an assault-gun brigade attached to them for anything more than a few days, so it was very difficult to build up a base of experience between the infantry regiments and attached assault-gun units. The Heer attempted to make up for the limited training opportunities by issuing small comic books called "*Fibel*," which presented the basic tactics in a clever

This view inside a StuG III Ausf G was taken from the commander's seat and shows the gunner's controls to the right, the 7.5cm StuK 40 gun in the center, and the loader's station to the right. (Author)

and amusing fashion. The *Fibel* dealing with infantry cooperation with tanks and assault guns was *Merkblatt 18b/38 'Panzer hilfen Dir: Was der Grenadier vom gepanzerten Kampffahrzeuge wissen muß' (Armor helps you: what the grenadier needs to know about tanks and assault guns).*

Three assault-gun brigades took part in the Übach-Palenberg battle described in the following chapter. All of these StuG III

The gun in the StuG III was aimed using a Selbstfahrlafetten Zielfernrohr Sfl ZF1a 5× periscopic sight. This is a view from the driver's station upward toward the gunner; the commander's open hatch can be seen behind. (NARA)

# StuG III FIGHTING COMPARTMENT

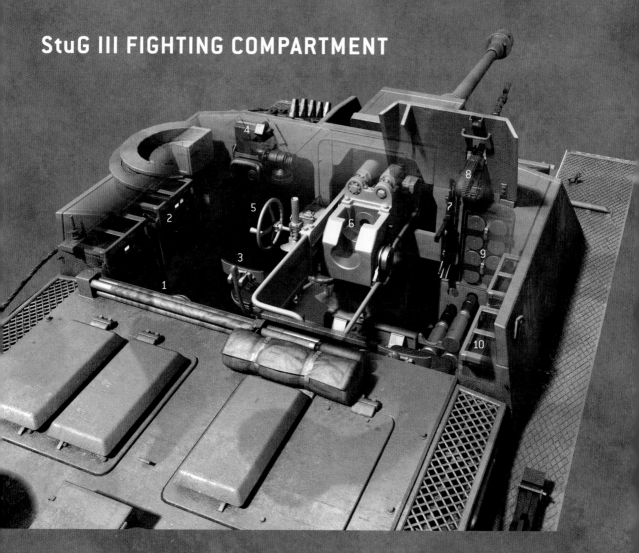

| | | | |
|---|---|---|---|
| **1** | Gun cleaning rods | **6** | 7.5cm StuK 40 gun |
| **2** | Left-side radio/intercom rack | **7** | MP 38 submachine gun |
| **3** | Gunner's seat | **8** | MG 34 machine gun |
| **4** | Selbstfahrlafetten Zielfernrohr Sfl ZF1a gunner's sight | **9** | Ammunition ready rack (forward) |
| **5** | Gunner's elevation wheel | **10** | Right-side radio rack |

## StuG III AMMUNITION

**1** 7.5cm PzGr 39 APCBC (armor piercing capped, ballistic cap)

**2** 7.5cm SprGr 34 HE (high explosive)

units had been formed and trained in France in 1943 and 1944 and had fought in Normandy. The Lehr- und Aufstellungsstab-West had been established at Camp du Ruchard south of Tours in 1943 to train new Sturmgeschütz units and to rebuild units that had become decimated on the Eastern Front.

The first of the three units under discussion was StuG-Brig 341. It was originally raised as "Kommando Greif" in Wehrkreis VIII in May 1943 and was dispatched to Tours in late November 1943 for training. It was one of the rare reinforced units with 45 assault guns, with an intended strength of 33 Stug III and 12 StuH 42. It began receiving its StuG III in March 1944 and received its final batch of 28 assault guns on July 1, 1944. After training, the unit was deployed with Heeresgruppe G in March 1944 in southern France and was stationed near Carcassonne through late July 1944. The brigade was one of a number of units transferred from southern France to reinforce the Normandy front in the desperate final weeks of July as the Normandy front was collapsing. Its first batteries were assigned to try to stop the Operation

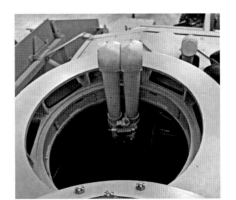

The StuG commander's main sighting equipment was a Scherenfahrlafetten SF 14Z scissors telescope on a fixed mount at the front of the cupola. There was also a set of eight periscopic sights for close-range observation. (Author)

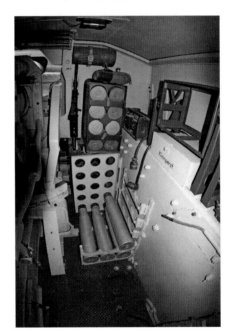

The loader in the StuG III Ausf G was stationed to the right of the gun with the main ammunition rack in front of him. He also operated the vehicle radio located in the right sponson; in this restored StuG III Ausf G of Jacques Littlefield's MVTF museum, the radio is not fitted, though the mounting frame can be seen. (Author)

The crew of the StuG III Ausf G was concentrated in cramped conditions on the left side of the fighting compartment with the driver in the front followed by the gunner and commander. (Author)

*Cobra* breakout by the US VII Corps, and in the process 1./StuG-Brig 341 was largely destroyed, losing 12 of its 14 assault guns and its commander killed. The other batteries were committed to the fighting near Saint-Malo. By the middle of August, the brigade was part of the general retreat from France and was re-equipped with about 20 assault guns when it reached Fontainebleau near Paris. By the time the brigade has retreated to the Aachen area at the beginning of September, it had been reduced to about a dozen operational assault guns and had lost all three of its battery commanders either killed or captured. The brigade underwent rebuilding in

September and command was taken over by Hauptmann Erich Barkley, an Eastern Front veteran from Sturmgeschütz-Batterie 660. The unit's three batteries were scattered between the Aachen area and the Luxembourg frontier and by the end of September, 1./StuG-Brig 341 was stationed west of Jülich and the remainder of the brigade was attached to the 276. Infanterie-Division further north. It had ten StuG III operational and 13 in repair on October 1, and was awaiting delivery of 17 StuH 42.

The second of the units began as the Sturmgeschütz-Aufstellungs- und Lehr-Abteilung Tours in January 1944, becoming the Tours training unit. It was converted to a regular assault-gun brigade, StuG-Brig 902, on June 1, 1944, and following the D-Day landings it was directed to reinforce the LXXXIV. Armeekorps in Normandy against US units. It saw extensive combat in July during the fighting on the approaches to Saint-Lô, and took heavy losses during the Operation *Cobra* breakout. By August 1, it had lost 20 of its 31 assault guns and many of the remainder were in repair. The shattered remnants of the brigade, reduced to six assault guns, reached German soil by early September and were directed to Bütgenbach for rebuilding under a new commander, Major Georg Kaiser. For much of September, the unit was broken up and bounced around from corps to corps, finally ending up with the LXXXI. Armeekorps by the end of the month. On October 1, 1944, it had a strength of 19 operational assault guns and one in repair, and on October 3 it received a shipment of 12 StuH 42.

The third of the brigades to take part in this battle was StuG-Brig 394, which had been raised in March 1944 in Wehrkreis XX and then sent to Tours for training. Prior to the D-Day landings, it was stationed in the Cher region of France and was ordered to the Normandy front on the night of July 30/31. It took part in the fighting near Mortain and Avranches in early August and its 3. Batterie claimed to have knocked out 26 Shermans during the fighting on August 6, 1944. The brigade commander, Hauptmann von Jena, claimed six Shermans destroyed and he was later decorated with the German Cross in Gold for the skirmish. The brigade became trapped in the Falaise Pocket, but about 350 of its troops escaped the pocket near Saint-Germain with only a single assault gun. The remnants of the unit were assembled in the Aachen area and after receiving new assault guns, its separate batteries were sent into action in support of Pz-Brig 105 and the 9. Panzer-Division in the first battle of Aachen in mid-September 1944. As of October 1, 1944, it had 16 StuG III and nine StuH 42 operational and seven more in repair.

Besides the three StuG III brigades in the Aachen area in October 1944, there were a number of other units equipped with assault guns. The most unusual assault-gun unit was the Pz-Kp(Fkl) 319, which operated the remote-controlled Borgward B IV demolition vehicles. The companies used StuG III equipped with special radios to direct the B IV to their targets. Their nominal strength was a set of 36 demolition vehicles and ten StuG III, and Pz-Kp(Fkl) 319 had 26 demolition vehicles and six StuG III in early October.

One of the more futuristic uses of the StuG III was as a command vehicle for the Borgward B IV remote-controlled demolition vehicle. This is a rare view of Panzer-Kompanie (Funklenk) 314 in action at Kursk on the Eastern Front in July 1943 when it was supporting the attempts by the 2. Panzer-Division to breach Soviet defensive minefields. (NARA)

# M10

## CREW

The M10 had a crew of five: gun commander, gunner, assistant gunner (loader), driver, and assistant driver. The gun commander was positioned on the right side of the turret and directed the rest of the crew. He observed the terrain either from within the protective armor of the turret using the periscopic telescope, or could stand up above the turret opening and observe the terrain using binoculars. The gun commander was connected to the rest of the crew via the vehicle intercom system. The gunner sat in the left side of the turret and operated the gun using the telescopic sight for direct fire, and two manual hand-wheels for traverse and elevation. Behind him was the assistant gunner whose main responsibility was loading the gun; his secondary responsibility was the antiaircraft machine gun. The driver sat in the left front of the vehicle and observed the terrain either through a periscopic sight when in combat, or by opening the hatch above him and elevating the seat for a clearer view when outside the combat zone. The assistant driver was a leftover from the M10's origins with the Sherman tank. Since tank destroyers lacked the bow machine gun found on medium tanks, this crewman's responsibility was limited to operating the vehicle radio. In the case of combat casualties, this position was left vacant.

The thin frontal armor of the M10 led to various field improvisations. AFVs in the Ninth US Army often had this particular style consisting of a layer of spare track links welded to the front followed by sandbags and a camouflage net. Here, three M10 tank destroyers are seen advancing through München-Gladbach on March 1, 1945 when the town was captured by the US 29th Division during Operation *Grenade*. (NARA)

# M10 TURRET

1  3in ammunition ready rack (left side)
2  Gunner's traverse handwheel
3  Gunner's M70G telescopic sight
4  Gun travel lock
5  M12 panoramic artillery telescope

6  3in M7 gun in M5 mount
7  Folding brace for turret roof tarp
8  .45-caliber submachine gun
9  3in ammunition ready rack (right side)

# M10 AMMUNITION

1  3in M42A1 HE (high explosive)
2  3in M62A1 APC (armor piercing capped)

## US TANK-DESTROYER BATTALIONS

M10 battalions were organized under TO&E 18-35 and consisted of a headquarters company, reconnaissance company, and three tank-destroyer companies; they included 36 tank destroyers, six M8 armored cars, 30 M20 armored cars, and three M32 tank-recovery vehicles. The tank-destroyer companies included a company headquarters and three platoons, with each platoon having four M10 tank destroyers, a jeep, and two M20 armored cars for reconnaissance, for a total of 12 M10 tank destroyers per company. One of the most significant difference between the US and German tables of equipment was that the US units were generally at or near full strength while the German units in the fall of 1944 were usually substantially under strength.

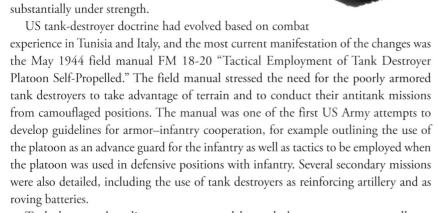

US tank-destroyer doctrine had evolved based on combat experience in Tunisia and Italy, and the most current manifestation of the changes was the May 1944 field manual FM 18-20 "Tactical Employment of Tank Destroyer Platoon Self-Propelled." The field manual stressed the need for the poorly armored tank destroyers to take advantage of terrain and to conduct their antitank missions from camouflaged positions. The manual was one of the first US Army attempts to develop guidelines for armor–infantry cooperation, for example outlining the use of the platoon as an advance guard for the infantry as well as tactics to be employed when the platoon was used in defensive positions with infantry. Several secondary missions were also detailed, including the use of tank destroyers as reinforcing artillery and as roving batteries.

The crew layout of the M10 was essentially similar to that in most tanks with a driver and assistant driver in the forward hull and the loader, gunner, and commander in the turret. (Author)

Tank-destroyer battalions were managed by tank-destroyer groups, usually on a scale of one tank-destroyer group per corps. This reflected the original idea of keeping the tank-destroyer battalions in corps reserve until a Panzer attack materialized and then the battalions would rush to staunch the breakthrough. At the time of the D-Day landings, the plans were to attach the towed tank-destroyer battalions to the infantry divisions directly, but to keep the self-propelled battalions concentrated at corps level. This plan quickly changed when infantry divisions began complaining that they needed a self-propelled assault gun for fire support due to the overwhelming disadvantages of the towed 3in guns. The towed guns could not fire over the hedgerows in Normandy, they were largely static once emplaced, and their thin armor shields made them very vulnerable. As a result, the self-propelled battalions were gradually assigned to the infantry divisions, especially those earmarked for offensive operations. As a result, the tank-destroyer group simply acted as an administrative headquarters, with the group commander usually serving as the tank-destroyer adviser to the corps headquarters. By the late summer of 1944, most US infantry divisions in the ETO had a separate tank and tank-destroyer battalion attached during offensive operations. During the Übach-Palenberg battles covered in the Combat chapter below, there were two M10 battalions attached to XIX Corps, as well as a towed 3in battalion.

The 702nd TD Battalion saw extensive combat in Normandy in the summer of 1944. One of the battalion's heavily camouflaged M10s is seen here on a roadblock near Domfront on August 16, 1944, a few days after heavy AFV fighting around Tessy-sur-Vire. (NARA)

In the case of the 30th Division, the 743rd Tank Battalion and the 823rd TD Battalion had been attached since the fighting in Normandy earlier in the summer. The 823rd TD Battalion was equipped with towed 3in antitank guns, but this configuration had recognized shortcomings during offensive operations. So for the October offensive the 803rd TD Battalion, equipped with M10 3in GMC, was also attached. Although US armored divisions did not have an organic tank-destroyer battalion, most divisions had one attached for most of the 1944–45 campaign. In the case of the 2nd Armored Division, it was the 702nd TD Battalion, also equipped with the M10 3in GMC.

The 702nd TD Battalion had been raised in December 1941 at Fort Benning, Georgia as a heavy battalion from a cadre of the 2nd Armored Division. The battalion was equipped with the M3 75mm GMC heavy tank destroyer and in January 1943 was transferred to the Tank Destroyer Center at Camp Hood, Texas for advanced training. In May 1943, it moved again to Camp Gruber in Oklahoma where it trained with the 42nd and 88th divisions. After participating in summer war games in Louisiana, the battalion was alerted in the fall of 1943 for overseas movement and exchanged its old half-tracks for the new M18 76mm GMC. Curiously enough, when it disembarked in Scotland in late February 1944, it was re-equipped with the M10 3in GMC and dispatched to Tidworth Barracks in England alongside the

2nd Armored Division to which it was attached. The battalion landed on Omaha Beach on June 11, 1944 and first saw extensive combat in early July 1944 during the fighting on the Cotentin peninsula. During the months of July through September 1944, the battalion suffered 178 casualties, including 33 killed and 145 wounded or about 20 percent of the unit's strength. In fact, casualties among the tank-destroyer crews were heavier than this would suggest, since most of the battalion casualties fell on the 180 crewmen of the M10 tank destroyers. The battalion claimed to have destroyed 38 German AFVs, mainly PzKpfw IV and Panther tanks; several M10s were damaged but none totally lost. By the time of the October fighting, the 702nd TD Battalion was battle-hardened and had been well integrated into the operations of the 2nd Armored Division.

The 803rd TD Battalion had initially been activated on September 30, 1940 as the 103rd Antitank Battalion from Washington National Guard troops, federalized on February 10, 1941, and redesignated as the 803rd TD Battalion on December 12, 1941 at Fort Lewis, Washington. Like the 702nd TD Battalion, it was equipped with M3 75mm GMC prior to overseas movement to England in July 1943. After landing in France on June 13, 1944 it was subordinated to the 2nd TD Group. The battalion saw very little combat during the summer months, and was temporarily attached to several divisions during the Normandy campaign before being attached to the

The 3in gun in the M10 was aimed either using the coaxial telescopic sight to the left of the gun mount for direct firing, or the artillery-type panoramic sight fitted to the right turret wall. (NARA)

49

The SCR-610 radio was located in the right front hull of the M10 and was operated by the assistant driver. (NARA)

30th Division prior to the Siegfried Line campaign. Another issue degrading the utility of the battalion in October 1944 was its dispersion; only two of its companies were committed to the fighting, while Company A was on detached duty in support of the 1st Belgian Brigade.

The tank-destroyer units attached to infantry divisions were usually deployed in a dispersed fashion. The after-action report by the 803rd TD Battalion recalled that:

> To facilitate closer cooperation and faster employment, one company was put in close support of each of the assaulting infantry regiments. Contrary to normal Tank Destroyer tactics, the company was broken down and a platoon was placed in close support of each infantry battalion. This variance from normal doctrine is essential when TDs are employed in a tank mission. The infantry must have direct fire support. It is emphasized that the tank destroyer company when used in its proper role can contribute considerably toward destroying the numerous enemy counterattacks. It should never be used to seek out enemy tanks that are definitely located.

The towed tank destroyers of the 823rd TD Battalion were not especially useful in offensive operations and during this battle they were subordinate to the 30th Division artillery and used mainly in the indirect field-artillery role.

# THE STRATEGIC SITUATION

## PENETRATING THE SCHARNHORST LINE, OCTOBER 1944

The skirmish featured in this study took place when the XIX Corps of the First US Army penetrated the Scharnhorst Line on October 2–9, 1944 – part of a broader scheme to complete the encirclement and capture of the city of Aachen. Defending this sector was the LXXXI. Armeekorps of the German AOK 7 (Seventh Army). The First US Army had penetrated through the Siegfried Line to the southeast of Aachen in early September before the Wehrmacht had been able to rejuvenate the abandoned fortification line. The "first battle of Aachen" in the last two weeks of September was fought primarily in the Aachen–Stolberg corridor to the south of the city. These battles were the opening phase that the US Army later dubbed the Siegfried Line campaign. The terrain in the battle zone was a mixture of open fields densely interspersed with industrial towns and extensive coal mining. The weather in early October was wet and cold, and the ground sodden from early fall rains.

As Aachen was the first German city to be threatened in the West, Hitler was adamant that it be held at all costs. On September 16, Hitler issued a Führer directive: there was no room for strategic maneuver now that the enemy had reached

The German defenses along the Wurm River depended on the pre-war Westwall fortification line that had been hastily rejuvenated in September 1944. These bunkers were a primary target of the US tank destroyers in the early October fighting. This particular bunker in Palenberg has been struck numerous times by weapons of different calibers. (NARA)

German soil: "Every man was to stand fast or die at his post." German Panzer reserves in the West had already been committed earlier in the month to other sectors, notably around Arnhem in the Netherlands to repulse the Allied airborne *Market Garden* operation, and in Lorraine against Patton's aggressive Third US Army assault. A number of badly battered Panzer units were thrown into the Aachen fight, including the 9. Panzer-Division, 116. Panzer-Division, and a number of smaller units including several StuG formations.

The "Siegfried Line" was the Allied misnomer for the West-Stellung: this was a combination of the old Westwall as well as a new fortification program started in August 1944 to deepen the original defenses.[5] The Wehrmacht had largely abandoned the Westwall defenses after the fall of France in 1940. There was a belated effort to reactivate the defenses in August 1944, but the specialized fortification units (Festung-Abteilungen) had been disbanded and many bunkers had been stripped of armament and equipment for the extravagant and wasteful Atlantikwall effort. The Westwall in the Aachen sector was unusually dense, with the Scharnhorst Line (Scharnhorst-Stellung) forward of the city, and the Schill Line behind Aachen.

---

5   For further details on the West-Stellung defenses, see Steven J. Zaloga, *Defense of the Rhine 1944–45*, Osprey Fortress 102.

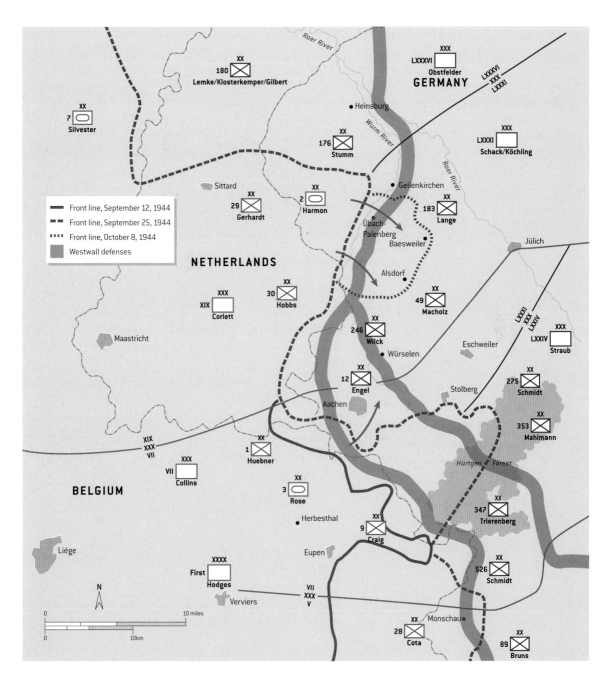

Legend:
- Front line, September 12, 1944
- Front line, September 25, 1944
- Front line, October 8, 1944
- Westwall defenses

Roer River

GERMANY

XXX LXXXVI Obstfelder

LXXXVI / XXX / LXXXI

Heinsburg

XX 180 Lemke/Klosterkemper/Gilbert

XX 7 Silvester

Wurm River

XX 176 Stumm

Roer River

XXX LXXXI Schack/Köchling

Sittard

XX 29 Gerhardt

XX 2 Harmon

Geilenkirchen

XX 183 Lange

Jülich

NETHERLANDS

Übach-Palenberg

Baesweiler

Alsdorf

XXX XIX Corlett

XX 30 Hobbs

XX 49 Macholz

LXXXI / XXX / LXXIV

Maastricht

XX 246 Wilck

Würselen

Eschweiler

XXX LXXIV Straub

XX 12 Engel

Aachen

Stolberg

XX 275 Schmidt

XX 353 Mahlmann

Hürtgen Forest

XXX / XXX / VII

XXX VII Collins

XX 1 Huebner

XX 3 Rose

BELGIUM

Herbesthal

XX 9 Craig

Eupen

XX 347 Trierenberg

Liége

XXXX First Hodges

Verviers

VII / XXX / V

XX 526 Schmidt

XX 28 Cota

Monschau

XX 89 Bruns

N

0    10 miles
0    10km

By the early fall of 1944, the Wehrmacht was recovering from its rout in Normandy. The German forces had been in headlong retreat through most of August and early September 1944, a period that German commanders called "the Void." By the middle of September, the Wehrmacht began to recover its strength. Numerous new units had been built up hastily in August and September 1944 and were thrown into the fighting. Many Luftwaffe and Kriegsmarine units had been disbanded due to fuel shortages caused by the Allied bomber campaign, and these personnel were put together in slapdash infantry units and sent to the Aachen front.

Encircling Aachen, September 12–October 8, 1944

# US PLANS

The two main options for Major General Charles "Cowboy Pete" Corlett's US XIX Corps for the October fighting were to push over the Wurm River on the north side of Aachen through the fortified Westwall, or to seize Geilenkirchen further to the north in the hopes of securing a major road network eastward. US Army intelligence concluded that the Geilenkirchen sector was too heavily fortified and too strongly defended, so planning focused on crossing the Wurm River. German units had reoccupied the Westwall defenses along the Scharnhorst Line on the eastern side of the Wurm River by the end of September, so a deliberate assault would be needed at the outset of the attack. To deflect German attention away from the actual target area, the First US Army staged "demonstrations" by other infantry divisions in the days before the actual attack to convince the Wehrmacht that the main blow would come elsewhere.

The initial attack to penetrate the Scharnhorst Line was assigned to the experienced 30th Division. Once the infantry had secured a firm bridgehead over the Wurm River, the 2nd Armored Division would commit one of its combat commands to exploit the penetration towards the northeast, while at the same time the 30th Division would turn south and complete the envelopment towards Aachen's northern suburbs. Due to the large number of bunkers in this sector, the XIX Corps attack was heavily reinforced with both artillery and armor.

The 30th Division engaged in extensive pre-attack training to develop specialized tactics for dealing with the Siegfried Line bunkers. Two specialized weapons were issued – man-portable flame-throwers and demolition charges mounted on poles to attack the vulnerable embrasures. Supporting tank and tank-destroyer units were also trained in bunker-busting tactics, with some tanks being fitted with flame-throwers in place of the hull machine gun. There was no expectation that tank or tank-destroyer guns could actually penetrate the thick concrete of the Westwall bunkers, but the training emphasized their role in suppressing German bunkers by firing at their embrasures. In addition, tank and tank-destroyer crews were trained in other bunker reduction tactics, including the use of smoke to assist the advance of infantry and engineer bunker-busting teams.

The XIX Corps began a concerted campaign to bombard the German bunkers with divisional artillery to damage the supporting field entrenchments and strip away camouflage from the bunkers. A number of M12 155mm GMC self-propelled guns of the 258th Field Artillery Battalion were moved up close to the Wurm River under the cover of darkness, and set about attacking the bunkers from a few hundred yards away. The XIX Corps attack was preceded by a major air attack by medium bombers of the Ninth Air Force, but the October 2 bombing had little effect on German fortifications already inundated by artillery over the past week.

# GERMAN PLANS

The focus of the AOK 7 defenses in the Aachen sector had been the contested Aachen–Stolberg corridor and most of the modest Panzer reserves were pushed into that sector. The area along the Wurm River had been relatively quiet and so the defenses were adequate but not especially dense. German commanders were anticipating another American push in early October. However, their assessment of the likely focus of the attack was mistaken. The commander of the LXXXI. Armeekorps, General der Infanterie Friedrich Köchling, believed that the main thrust would continue to be in the US VII Corps sector up the Aachen–Stolberg corridor. The commander of the 183. Volkgrenadier-Division, Generalleutnant Wolfgang Lange, expected that the main blow would fall on Geilenkirchen, and so he placed his small Panzer reserve, the 2.(StuG)/PzJg-Abt 1219, in that sector. This company, equipped with new Jagdpanzer 38(t), had only arrived at the end of September and its new equipment proved mechanically troublesome.

At the start of the October 1944 fighting, the LXXXI. Armeekorps deployed four infantry divisions. From north to south, they were the 183. Volksgrenadier-Division, the 49. Infanterie-Division, the 246. Volksgrenadier-Division, and the 12. Volksgrenadier-Division. The 12. Volksgrenadier-Division was assigned to the defense of Aachen itself. During this period of the war, German infantry divisions were supposed to include a tank-destroyer battalion with one company of 7.5cm PaK 40 of either the towed or self-propelled variety, and an assault-gun company equipped with 14 assault guns. In the case of the four divisions around Aachen, only two, the 12. and 183. Volksgrenadier-Divisionen, had an assault-gun company; the 12. Volksgrenadier-Division's 2.(StuG)/PzJg-Abt 12 had ten StuG IV while the 183. Volksgrenadier-Division's 2.(StuG)/PzJg-Abt 1219 had 14 Jagdpanzer 38(t).

Besides the divisional StuG companies, the LXXXI. Armeekorps had five assault-gun units assigned to it: StuG-Brig 341, 394, and 902, Pz-Kp(Fkl) 319, and StuPz-Abt 217. The initial strength of the StuG units at the beginning of October was 67 StuG and StuH 42 assault guns plus 19 Sturmpanzer IV Brummbär, far below their intended strength.

Due to the very thin defenses in the Aachen sector, the LXXXI. Armeekorps usually assigned the StuG III units to the infantry divisions. In early October, the bulk of the assault-gun units were concentrated around Aachen due to the recent fighting. Only a handful of Panzer units were in the sector targeted by the American attack. The 2.(StuG)/PzJg-Abt 1219 of the 183. Volksgrenadier-Division was located in reserve around Süggerath to the east of Geilenkirchen in the northern sector of the front, and a company of six Sturmpanzer IV Brummbär of StuPz-Abt 217 was in reserve with the 49. Infanterie-Division in the area between Baesweiler and Oidtweiler.

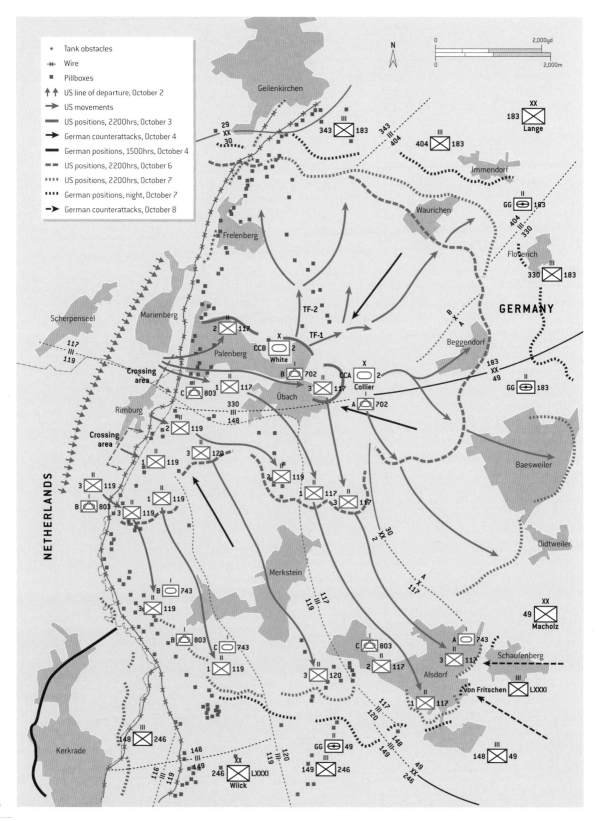

## Legend

* ★ Tank obstacles
* ✳ Wire
* ▪ Pillboxes
* ⬆⬆ US line of departure, October 2
* ➔ US movements
* ━ US positions, 2200hrs, October 3
* ➔ German counterattacks, October 4
* ━ German positions, 1500hrs, October 4
* - - US positions, 2200hrs, October 6
* ···· US positions, 2200hrs, October 7
* ···· German positions, night, October 7
* - -➔ German counterattacks, October 8

N

0 — 2,000yd
0 — 2,000m

Geilenkirchen

183 XX Lange

29 XX 30

343 III 183

343 III 404

404 III 183

Immendorf

GG II 183

Frelenberg

Waurichen

404 III 330

Floverich

330 III 183

Scherpenseel

Marienberg

2 II 117

TF-2

B X A

GERMANY

Palenberg

CCB X 2 White

TF-1

Beggendorf

Crossing area

117 III 119

C III 803

1 II 117

B III 702

CCA X 2 Collier

3 II 117

183 XX 49

GG II 183

Rimburg

330 III 148

Übach

A III 702

Crossing area

2 II 119

3 II 120

2 II 119

1 II 117 3 II 117

Baesweiler

3 II 119

1 II 119

B III 803

3 II 119

Oidtweiler

30 XX 2

NETHERLANDS

Merkstein

B I 743

3 II 119

A X 117

49 XX Macholz

B III 803

C I 743

C II 803 2 II 117

A II 743

3 II 117

Schaufenberg

1 II 119

3 II 120

Alsdorf

1 II 117

Von Fritschen III LXXXI

117 III 119

117 120

148 III 49

Kerkrade

148 III 246

148 III 149

GG II 49

149 III 246

148 III 149

49 XX 246

116 III 119

246 XX LXXXI Wilck

119 III 120

120 III 119

# COMBAT

## THE BATTLE FOR ÜBACH-PALENBERG

In order to deceive the Germans, a "demonstration" was conducted by the 29th Division in the pre-dawn hours near Geilenkirchen to draw away attention from the actual attack site. The 30th Division attack on the morning of October 2 was conducted by single battalions from two of its three regiments, the 117th and 119th Infantry. The river crossing was made using specially constructed footbridges. Resistance was modest and consisted mainly of machine-gun fire from surviving pillboxes and artillery fire directed from the bunkers. Some of the M10 tank destroyers were brought up near the river to provide direct fire support. By nightfall, the 117th Infantry was in control of the eastern portion of Palenberg.

Armored support for the original attack was supposed to come from the 743rd Tank Battalion and 803rd TD Battalion. Special expedient bridges were constructed by engineers before the attack consisting of concrete culverts wrapped in a protective cover of logs. These were mounted on special sleds that were pushed to the river-crossing sites by dozer tanks. The plan was to push the sled into the river and gradually create a bridge with the assistance of the dozer tanks. On the first day, this scheme failed when the dozer tanks and sleds became trapped in the mire near the river due to the soggy soil from recent rain. As a result, the tanks and M10 tank destroyers had to wait until late in the day until engineers had succeeded in establishing treadway bridges over the river.

Company A, 743rd Tank Battalion and Company C, 803rd TD Battalion moved across the bridge in the late afternoon and began to support the 117th Infantry

The Übach-Palenberg area was dominated by industrial zones and coalmines. Here, a heavily camouflaged M7 105mm HMC of the 2nd Armored Division is seen in the work-yard of the Carl-Alexander mine in Baesweiler. (NARA)

around Palenberg. The primary mission of the tank destroyers was to locate and destroy German observation posts that were directing the artillery fire against the bridgehead. Companies B and C, 743rd Tank Battalion and Company B, 803rd TD Battalion moved across the other treadway bridge near Rimburg, but several tanks became bogged down in the muddy soil of the opposite bank and only a portion of the tanks was able to advance.

The American attacks hit a delicate spot in the German defensive line, the boundary between the 183. Volksgrenadier-Division and the 49. Infanterie-Division. Generalleutnant Lange at first believed that the feint by the 29th Division near Geilenkirchen represented the real attack. When reports began to come in from the forward bunkers along the Wurm River, it became clear that the attacks towards Übach-Palenberg were the main thrust. Only a single infantry regiment was available in divisional reserve, and it was thrown into the fray with little effect. Lange wanted to reinforce the counterattack with his limited armor, but he was afraid that if the Jagdpanzer 38(t) company attempted to move in the daylight, it would be overwhelmed by air attack. As a result, the 2.(StuG)/PzJg-Abt 1219 did not begin its movement from the Geilenkirchen area until after dark. The night counterattack started three hours late, around 0030hrs on October 3, from a start point north of Rimburg towards Castle Palenberg. Several Jagdpanzer 38(t) followed behind the infantry battalion, but the attack was halted by heavy American artillery fire in the pre-dawn hours. Three Jagdpanzer 38(t) were lost in the fighting. Lange ordered the force to halt until a more substantial counterattack force could be built up. This Jagdpanzer 38(t) company was badly beaten up in the initial fighting both due to combat damage and breakdowns; later on October 4 it had only two vehicles operational and nine more in short-term repair.

The attacking American force was further enlarged on October 3 when Colonel Sidney Hinds' Task Force 2 (TF-2) of Combat Command B (CCB) of the 2nd Armored Division moved across the treadway bridges to help the 117th Infantry in its assault on Übach. The combat commands were combined-arms teams formed by mixing tank, armored infantry, armored artillery, and armored engineer units. In turn, the combat commands were broken down into smaller task forces that combined smaller tank and armored infantry units. In the case of CCB, the core of the unit was the 67th Armored Regiment operating with a battalion from the 41st Armored Infantry Regiment mounted on armored half-tracks, the 17th Armored Engineers, and the 78th Armored Field Artillery Battalion equipped with M7 105mm self-propelled howitzers. The two task forces each consisted of roughly a battalion of tanks, a few companies of armored infantry, a platoon of engineers, and a battery of self-propelled howitzers. The advance guard of each task force also had a company of M10 tank destroyers from the 702nd TD Battalion.

### OVERLEAF – Assault toward Beggendorf, October 6, 1944

Some of the most intense fighting between the StuG III and US armored units during the October Übach-Palenberg battle took place on October 6 when Combat Command B tried to push further to the northeast out of Übach and towards Beggendorf. Facing them was a gepanzerte Gruppe, the consolidated armored elements supporting the 183. Volksgrenadier-Division. This included 15 StuG III and six StuH 42 of StuG-Brig 394 and Pz-Kp(Fkl) 319, as well as the division's seven Jagdpanzer 38(t) and several Sturmpanzer IV Brummbär for a total of over two dozen assault guns of various types. The German assault guns were positioned on the edges of the towns and in the countryside between. Besides the assault guns, there were also numerous towed antitank guns and antitank rocket launchers of the associated infantry.

During the course of the day's fighting, LXXXI. Armeekorps claimed to have knocked out 41 US tanks and claimed mobility kills on a further 11. Actual losses in CCB were five tanks lost. A further 13 tanks were disabled by enemy action or mechanical problems, but subsequently recovered. Combat Command A, 2nd Armored Division was brought in to reinforce the attack, and Companies A and C of the 702nd TD Battalion served in the CCA attack. Company A claimed to have knocked out two German assault guns. Company C took part in the attack on Beggendorf. The battalion suffered its heaviest losses of the battle on this day, with one M10 a total loss and three more disabled but later recovered. German losses were three vehicles, a Jagdpanzer 38(t), a StuG III, and a StuH 42.

This illustration shows an engagement between StuG-Brig 394 and elements of the 702nd TD Battalion outside Beggendorf. The German assault guns generally engaged from overwatch positions since their limited traverse was a tactical liability at close ranges. This was based on a lesson learned by most armored units during World War II – the unit which sees first, engages first, and hits first usually gains the tactical edge in armored skirmishes.

An M8 75mm HMC of the Headquarters, 3rd Battalion, 67th Armored Regiment, 2nd Armored Division crosses the railway tracks near the Palenberg station on October 4, 1944, shortly after Combat Command B was committed to the Übach-Palenberg fighting. (NARA)

As it became apparent that the attack on Übach-Palenberg represented the main American assault, General der Infanterie Köchling's LXXXI. Armeekorps agreed to reinforce the 183. Volksgrenadier-Division counterattack. It first transferred the Sturmpanzer IV company of the StuPz-Abt 217 previously attached to the 49. Infanterie-Division to Lange's control and later in the day moved StuG-Brig 341 and 902 from Aachen to Lange's command. The counterattack force eventually consisted of five infantry and engineer battalions under Hauptmann Schrader and elements of four assault-gun units – StuG-Brig 902, StuG-Brig 341, StuG-Abt 1183, and StuPz-Abt 217 – under Hauptmann Barkley of StuG-Brig 341.

The intention was to launch the counterattack from the Merkstein–Alsdorf area northward, but it proved difficult to assemble the force. Instead of striking a concentrated blow, the attack degenerated into a series of small, disjointed assaults. The initial attack was launched around 0215hrs on October 4 by the divisional engineer battalion, Pionier-Bataillon 219, which managed to push into Übach with the help of a few StuG III. The first major commitment of Barkley's assault-gun force came around dawn when the StuG III of StuG-Brig 341 and StuG-Brig 902 supported an infantry-battalion attack through the woods south of Rimburg. Several StuG III "came down the road leading northwest into the woods spraying machine-gun fire into the American positions and Company I , 119th Infantry was forced back," according to the 30th Division account. The German infantry attack was brought to a halt when hit by tree-bursts by their own artillery and finally pushed back by a US counterattack. The StuG III pulled back and continued firing on US positions through the early-morning hours. Another attack by three infantry battalions supported by 2.(StuG)/PzJg-Abt 1219 and StuPz-Abt 217 was halted before it got under way by intense US artillery bombardment.

In the meantime, TF-1 of CCB began moving over the Palenberg treadway bridges and advanced into Übach. Company G, 67th Armored Regiment was ordered to push east out of Übach towards Beggendorf, a mission widely considered suicidal because of the German antitank guns and artillery covering the open ground between the two towns. An armored skirmish erupted when the two US tank platoons were engaged by seven StuG III. In the ensuing fight, three StuG III were claimed for the loss of two M4 medium tanks.

Soldiers of a rifle platoon of 1/41st Armored Infantry advance behind an M4 medium tank in the outskirts of Übach during the attempt on October 6, 1944 by the 2nd Armored Division's CCB to advance beyond the town. (NARA)

The commitment of the American armored division was deeply worrying to senior German commanders, who feared that it could lead to a breakthrough in the Aachen sector. On the morning of October 4, the German front commander, Generalfeldmarshall Gerd von Rundstedt, and the AOK 7 commander, General der Panzertruppen Erich Brandenberger, both arrived at Köchling's LXXXI. Armeekorps command post to survey the situation. They concluded that the corps did not have the resources to crush the attack and determined to rush all available forces into the sector. The forces immediately available were not especially impressive, and mostly involved transferring forces from the Aachen area to the threatened sector further north. Instead of a single counterattack force based on Lange's 183. Volksgrenadier-Division, Köchling decided to reinforce Generalleutnant Siegfried Macholz's 49. Infanterie-Division to shield the northern suburbs of Aachen. Armored reinforcements included StuG-Brig 394 and the assault guns of Pz-Kp(Fkl) 319. Brandenberger's only remaining Panzer reserve, the 33 Tiger II tanks of sPz-Abt 506, was also ordered into the sector. Brandenberger was very critical of the previous use of the assault guns by the LXXXI. Armeekorps and in particular Köchling's reluctance to move the units during daylight hours for fear of air attack. He instructed Köchling to maneuver the assault guns in daylight regardless of American air activity.

This M10 3in GMC of Company B, 803rd TD Battalion was knocked out while supporting the 119th Infantry during the fighting in Übach on October 4–6. There is a large-caliber hit visible on the differential cover and glacis plate. This vehicle is fitted with an additional .30-caliber machine gun on the front of the turret roof, a more practical location than the standard mount for the .50-caliber heavy machine gun at the turret rear. It has also been modified with a T3 "Rhino" hedge-cutter on the bow. (NARA)

Although Köchling had intended to stage another major counterattack on the night of October 4/5, the delays in moving the reinforcements into the Übach area stymied these plans. The US offensive continued all along the perimeter with a new push to the south that engulfed Merkstein. German attempts to regain Merkstein led to bitter fighting all day long. As German reinforcements arrived, they were plugged into the line in hopes of restraining the American advance. By the evening of October 5, the Heeresgruppe B commander, Generalfeldmarschall Walter Model, instructed Köchling to disregard his plans of a counterattack and simply focus on holding the existing line. The prominent role played by American tanks in facilitating the offensive prompted Model to issue special instructions to Köchling about the need for specialized tank-destroyer teams. These teams were to consist of one officer and 12 men armed with antitank rockets. The team would be organized into three sections, each equipped with a Kübelwagen for greater mobility.

Fighting in the Übach-Palenberg area took on a grim tactical monotony. Advances by US tank–infantry teams were met first by artillery fire and then by infantry counterattacks, sometimes supported by a few assault guns. The German counterattacks were beaten up by heavy American artillery and tank fire, and then the process began all over again. Both sides commented on the intensity of artillery fire in their reports. The 30th Division recorded that German artillery in the Übach-Palenberg battle was the heaviest it had ever experienced; this division had already gone through the fury of the Saint-Lô fighting in July. Likewise, the LXXXI. Armeekorps found the level of American artillery fire to be daunting; German records estimate the average daily expenditure in the fighting to have been 3,000 rounds on the German side and 10,700 on the American side.

By the evening of October 5, German armored strength around the American salient had been badly reduced by the continual fighting. Aside from a few vehicles lost in direct combat, the wet fall weather led to deep mud in some sectors causing numerous vehicle breakdowns. By that evening, the 183. Volksgrenadier-Division's operational Panzer contingent consisted of only nine StuG III, seven StuH 42, seven Jagdpanzer 38(t), and two Brummbär. Most of these were located around Beggendorf and Baesweiler in an effort to block CCB's exploitation to the east. The 49. Infanterie-Division was even weaker, with a paltry nine StuG III, located mainly in the Merkstein sector. American forces pushed into Beggendorf on October 5 and infantry losses on both sides were heavy.

Model visited Köchling at the corps headquarters again on the afternoon of October 5 to help plan a major counterattack. About the only armored reserve he could offer was the 2.(StuG)/PzJg-Abt 12 from the 12. Volksgrenadier-Division defending Aachen, which at the time had 9–10 StuG IV. Neither 183. Volksgrenadier-Division nor 49. Infanterie-Division had the strength to conduct any counterattacks. By October 7, the 183. Volksgrenadier-Division had a combat strength of fewer than a thousand infantrymen while 49. Infanterie-Division had only about 250 men. In view of the weakness of the 49. Infanterie-Division and its importance in shielding Aachen, Köchling was forced to transfer assault guns to 49. Infanterie-Division's control from Lange's 183. Volksgrenadier-Division. For any infantry counterattack to have a chance of success, support by a few assault guns was a vital enhancement to the morale of the beleaguered infantry.

The fighting on October 6 included one of the more unusual armored attacks of the campaign. The 2nd Battalion, 67th Armored Regiment continued the push beyond Übach and took heavy losses in the face of antitank guns and assault guns of the 183. Volksgrenadier-Division. After two days of fighting, the American battalion had 63 percent of its medium tanks destroyed, damaged, or in repair. In desperation, the battalion decided to use its light tank element, Company C, in a fast cavalry charge. At 1100hrs, the M5A1 light tanks raced forward and took the German defenders by surprise due to their speed. Amid the victims of the charge were three German assault guns. After penetrating through the defensive line, the light tanks ran into an advancing company of four tanks, claimed to be Tiger II heavy tanks of sPz-Abt 506. The heavy

### German LXXXI. Armeekorps AFV strength, October 7, 1944

**Gepanzerte Gruppe (183. Volksgrenadier-Division):**

| | |
|---|---|
| 2.(StuG)/PzJg-Abt 1219 | 4 Jagdpanzer 38(t) |
| StuG-Brig 394 | 4 StuG III, 5 StuH 42 |
| StuPz-Abt 217 | 3 Sturmpanzer IV |
| Pz-Kp(Fkl) 319 | 4 StuG III |

**Gepanzerte Gruppe Kaiser (49. Infanterie-Division):**

| | |
|---|---|
| StuG-Brig 902 | 9 StuG III |
| StuG-Brig 341 | 6 StuH 42 |
| 2.(StuG)/PzJg-Abt 12 | 7 StuG IV |

An M10 named "Burnside" of Company B, 702nd TD Battalion in a static position south of Geilenkirchen in early November 1944 after the fighting along the Scharnhorst Line. This vehicle has the intermediate wedge-shaped turret counterweights. (NARA)

tanks were hit numerous times with 37mm fire and withdrew. Deciding that their luck was running out, the M5A1 light tanks also withdrew, losing three of their number during the course of the day's fighting.

By the end of October 6, the 2nd Armored Division's CCB had only about half of its tanks operational. As a result, CCA was moved into the salient to reinforce the attack. CCA's central combat element was the 66th Armored Regiment and due to its weakness in infantry, it usually created task forces with infantry from the 30th Division. On the morning of October 7, CCA pushed out of the Übach salient in force and reached the outer edge of Baesweiler and Alsdorf. The force attacking Baesweiler had four vehicles disabled by antitank mines, including an M10 of the 702nd TD Battalion that was supporting the attack. Once the town was secured, CCA divided its resources into two task forces. TF Herkness, consisting of E/66th Armored Regiment and L/116th Infantry, was instructed to attack from Baesweiler southward toward Oidtweiler. The larger TF Parker, consisting of three tank companies of the 1/66th Armored Regiment, was instructed to approach Oidtweiler from the open fields between Baesweiler and Alsdorf.

By this stage of the fighting, most of the 14 assault guns operational under Lange's 183. Volkgrenadier-Division were deployed on the northern side of the American salient, facing CCB around Apweiler and Floverich. Generalmajor Macholz's 49. Infanterie-Division had 22 assault guns at the time, 18 of which were operational, deployed around Oidtweiler.

When CCA began moving south out of Baesweiler in the early afternoon, Macholz ordered his assault guns in Oidtweiler to launch an immediate counterattack. The StuG III units did not fight in the open, but followed their usual tactics of securing a good ambush site and engaging the advancing American tanks from cover. So, for example, the recently arrived 2.(StuG)/PzJg-Abt 12 with its seven StuG IV divided its force into two sections on either side of Oidtweiler with the vehicles in hull-down positions. Around 1400hrs, TF Herkness with about a dozen tanks made its way down the road from Baesweiler and was engaged by the section under Oberfähnrich Mallwitz, which claimed four tanks knocked out and two more hit. TF Herkness had one tank knocked out and claimed to have knocked out one of the German guns.

The larger TF Parker attacked Oidtweiler from west and south, with F/66th Armored attacking frontally, I/66th Armored attacking from the south, and C/66th Armored in reserve. The American tanks penetrated into the town and captured numerous prisoners. The accompanying Company A, 702nd TD Battalion claimed two of the German assault guns during the fighting that day. The StuG IV detachment under Feldwebel Luschmann claimed five US tanks knocked out; actual losses were two tanks. The infantry battalion defending the Oidtweiler sector, the II./Gren-Rgt 48, lost 178 of its original 270 men, thereby creating a critical gap in the German defenses.

With the defenses north of Aachen on the verge of collapse, AOK 7 finally agreed to major reinforcements including Pz-Brig 108. To conduct the counterattack, the schnelles (mobile) Regiment von Fritschen was moved from Luxembourg into the 49. Infanterie-Division sector. This bicycle-mobile unit included three fresh infantry battalions. Due to the heavy use of American tanks in this sector, a special tank-destroyer battalion was provided for the attack, Panzer-Zerstörungs-Bataillon AOK 7. This improvised unit was equipped mainly with Panzerfaust antitank rockets and some towed antitank guns. Armored support for the attack consisted of about 22 assault guns from the Gruppe Kaiser assigned to the 49. Infanterie-Division, and seven Panther tanks from the newly arrived Kampfgruppe Muskulus of Pz-Brig 108. Artillery support from at least a hundred guns was promised. Oberstleutnant von Fritschen was instructed that Alsdorf had to be retaken even if it cost every man in his regiment, otherwise Aachen would be lost. Alsdorf controlled one of the two main routes into Aachen from the north (the other route being via Mariadorf).

Köchling had planned to start the counterattack in the pre-dawn hours of October 8 to shield the regiment under the cover of darkness and early-morning mist against the American artillery observers. As was so often the case, Regiment von Fritschen arrived late and was not able to launch the attack until 0915hrs, by which time the morning mists had lifted and the infantry was exposed to American artillery observers. Some German soldiers mordantly observed that the attack across open ground was a hopeless "Charge of the Light Brigade." The attack on the left by Abt 504 of Regiment von Fritschen southeast of Alsdorf was stopped dead in its tracks by heavy American artillery fire, suffering 106 casualties. This force was supported by about 15 StuG III from StuG-Brig 341 and 902, but neither formation was able to contribute much to the attack when smothered by artillery fire. As a result, it fell upon the hapless Abt 506, also of Regiment von Fritschen, to conduct the main attack.

# THE RELUCTANT DRAGON OF ALSDORF

Regiment von Fritschen's main objective, the town of Alsdorf, had been occupied by the 1/117th and 3/117th Infantry of the 30th Division. Both battalions advanced out of Alsdorf at 0725hrs prior to the German attack, with the aim of capturing Mariadorf to the south. This infantry attack was spearheaded by tanks of Company A, 743rd Tank Battalion, with the 3rd Platoon attached to the 3/117th Infantry and the 1st and 2nd Platoons attached to the 1/117th Infantry. Company C, 803rd TD Battalion also took part in the attack, with its three platoons divided between the infantry battalions. The town of Alsdorf was left undefended except for the 3/117th Infantry's battalion headquarters, a platoon of infantry, and a single M10 tank destroyer.

While the American attack towards Mariadorf was taking place, Rittmeister Dunker's Abt 506 launched its own attack out of Schaufenberg against Alsdorf, supported by the StuG IV of 2./StuG-Abt 1012. Oberleutnant von Bitter's company had six assault guns at the start of the attack, but his own vehicle broke down almost immediately and he transferred to another vehicle. As the attacking German force approached Alsdorf, it was engaged by tanks of the 1st and 2nd Platoons, Company A, 743rd Tank Battalion. Three of the five StuG IV were knocked out, but the two others reached the cover of Alsdorf along with a few dozen infantrymen of Abt 506.

The main American force in Alsdorf was Lieutenant Colonel Samuel McDowell's 3/117th Infantry command post, located in a three-story school building at the edge of town. When the 3/117th Infantry realized the Germans were staging an attack on Alsdorf behind them, they radioed back to Lieutenant Colonel McDowell whether they should return to the town to repel the German attack. McDowell responded, "Hell no, you go ahead and secure Mariadorf, I can handle the situation here." The command post included a forward observer from the 118th Field Artillery Battalion, and he called in artillery strikes into the fields between Alsdorf and Schaufenberg. This prevented the bulk of Dunker's Abt 506 from reaching Alsdorf and caused heavy casualties among the exposed German infantry.

The two surviving StuG IV took up positions on the outskirts of Alsdorf, and began to fight their way into the town. The two vehicles were commanded by Feldwebel Peter Klimas and the company leader, Oberleutnant von Bitter. Klimas was the most highly decorated soldier in the company, having been awarded the German Cross in Gold in May 1944, and credited with knocking out 22 enemy tanks. His StuG IV was credited with knocking out two tanks the previous day in the fighting near Oidtsweiler. Klimas moved his StuG IV into the town, but was attacked by roving teams of US riflemen, some armed with bazookas. His StuG IV was dubbed "the Reluctant Dragon" by the US battalion staff who coordinated efforts to hunt it down. Klimas and his loader were wounded by a team of riflemen led by Lieutenant C. M. Spilman who had set up an ambush from an upper-story window. Klimas' StuG IV responded by firing at

The crew of an M4 medium tank of CCA, 2nd Armored Division, repairs a track with the help of an M31 tank-recovery vehicle in Alsdorf on October 15, 1944. The tank had hit a mine outside of town. (NARA)

the window, knocking Spilman down two flights of stairs but leaving him miraculously uninjured. The cat-and-mouse game continued in Alsdorf for most of the afternoon with neither side having enough power to secure the town. Kampfgruppe Muskulus, commanded by Oberstleutnant Friedrich Muskulus of Pz-Brig 108, attempted to intervene in the Alsdorf fighting in the afternoon, but soon encountered heavy American tank-gun fire in the open fields outside the town, and withdrew without having much effect.

In the meantime, the 2/117th Infantry, which had been in regimental reserve west of Alsdorf, was ordered forward to secure Alsdorf. Street fighting continued through the afternoon as the 2/117th Infantry pushed the weak remnants of Abt 506 out of the town around 1600hrs. The day's fighting had decimated Abt 506, which lost about half its force, including 29 killed, 226 missing, and 47 wounded. The two surviving StuG IV withdrew back to Schaufenberg by 1700hrs, with many of their crew wounded. During the fighting of the previous two days, the 2./StuG-Abt 1012 had four of its StuG IV destroyed and the remaining three seriously damaged. Klimas' exceptional performance in Alsdorf was later cited in dispatches with the note that "his performance deserves the highest praise."

During the initial stages of the attack, the StuG IV of 2./StuG-Abt 1012 were hit by tank fire from Co. A, 743rd Tank Battalion near Schaufenberg. This is one of the three vehicles knocked out in this fighting, seen in a rare photograph taken after the war. (Dieter Bast)

The failed attack of Regiment von Fritschen sealed the fate of Aachen. That same day, the US Army's VII Corps restarted its attack in the southern Aachen sector – so Köchling's LXXXI. Armeekorps now had two sectors to defend. The badly battered Sturmartillerie force north of Aachen dispersed yet again in a mad dash to reinforce the threatened Aachen–Stolberg corridor. The fighting around Alsdorf and Mariadorf on October 8–9 narrowed the gap between the two American corps to only a few miles. The attempted junction point of the "steel ring around Aachen" became the scene of the most intense fighting in the Aachen campaign, and lasted a week. The final encirclement of Aachen was not completed until October 16 and the city itself fell on October 21.

Following the attack by Regiment von Fritschen on October 8, the 823rd TD Battalion was instructed to move some of its towed M5 3in antitank guns forward to provide antitank defense after the 117th Infantry, 30th Division seized Schaufenberg on October 9. Alongside the gun are a bazooka team and a .50-caliber heavy machine gun. (NARA)

# STATISTICS AND ANALYSIS

The combat in the Aachen sector in early October 1944 was typical of the combat missions of the American M10 tank destroyers and German StuG III assault guns in this theater. Of the two types, the German assault guns undoubtedly played a more central part, if for no other reason than they made up the bulk of the AFVs available to LXXXI. Armeekorps. At the beginning of the fighting on October 2, all of the 80 German armored vehicles available to LXXXI. Armeekorps were assault guns of one type or another and the 50 StuG and StuH 42 amounted to three-quarters of the force. Even in the heavy fighting on October 8–9, the assault guns were the majority of the armored vehicles since German tank reinforcements to the sector were so paltry. The presence of assault guns was an essential ingredient in all major German counterattacks in the Übach-Palenberg battle. While the assault guns could not ensure victory, the only attacks where German infantry counterattacks managed to reoccupy captured towns, at Übach on October 4 and Alsdorf on October 8, were accomplished with armored support.

One of the main handicaps facing German assault-gun brigades was the lack of any tank–infantry training or communication. The standard assault-gun doctrine of keeping the assault guns together in brigade strength was routinely ignored, degrading their battlefield effectiveness. As can be deduced from the preceding account, AFV strength along the Westwall was so paltry that the corps commander was obliged to shift individual companies from one crisis to another, often arriving only hours before the start of a counterattack. The assault guns went into combat alongside infantry units with no prior contact. Furthermore, these recently rebuilt infantry formations

A column of M10s from Company A, 634th TD Battalion fight their way into the outskirts of Aachen on October 14, 1944 in support of the 1st "Big Red One" Infantry Division during the second battle for Aachen. These are late-production M10s with the enlarged turret and duck-bill counterweights. (NARA)

often had little or no experience in operating with AFVs. Elementary rules, such as not bunching up too closely to the assault guns, were routinely ignored by the inexperienced infantry. As a result, the infantry suffered significant casualties when the sound of the assault guns inevitably attracted US artillery fire. The assault-gun companies that were organic to the infantry divisions might have been better prepared than the separate brigades, but the Jagdpanzer 38(t)-equipped company in the 183. Volksgrenadier-Division, 2.(StuG)/PzJg-Abt 1219, had only arrived days before the start of the Übach-Palenberg fighting, and the company with the 49. Infanterie-Division, 2.(StuG)/PzJg-Abt 12, had come from the neighboring 12. Volksgrenadier-Division since it lacked its own organic company. Assault-gun employment in this fighting, as was typical of the fall 1944 campaign, often involved desperate measures under difficult circumstances. The assault guns no doubt contributed to small tactical victories won at great cost by the infantry, but their impact on the battle as a whole was negligible. US Army after-action reports from this battle frequently mention the effectiveness of German artillery, but seldom record any concern about German AFVs.

Armored losses in the October fighting on both sides were significant. LXXXI. Armeekorps records indicate that German AFV losses for October 1–10 were 45 in total, which was roughly half the starting force. At the same time, LXXXI. Armeekorps

units claimed to have knocked out 127 American tanks. Total US losses were over 40 AFVs consisting of 30 medium tanks, four light tanks, and ten M10 tank destroyers. However, a significant additional number of vehicles were knocked out, repaired, and put back into service. US tank and tank-destroyer units claimed to have knocked out at least 15 self-propelled guns and 20 tanks during this fighting and many of the "Mk IV tanks" claimed as knocked out were in fact German assault guns.

The disproportionate role of the StuG III and other assault guns in the fall 1944 fighting was evidence of the equipment problems facing the Wehrmacht in the West after the heavy tank losses in the summer campaign in Normandy. The relative balance between tanks and assault guns shifted after September 1944 due to the inability of the Wehrmacht rapidly to replace the heavy Normandy tank losses, as well as due to Hitler's insistence that the Panzer divisions be hoarded for the planned Ardennes offensive later in the year. While StuG strength remained the bedrock of German Westfront AFV strength in the fall months, tank strength waxed and waned depending on whether Hitler permitted local commanders to dip into the Ardennes Panzer reserve. So during November 1944, tank strength in the Aachen sector increased for a few weeks to rebuff the American Operation *Queen* offensive. The declining role of German tanks in the fall campaigning is apparent when comparing German AFV casualties. (The September losses are included in the summer Normandy figures because German statistics delayed incorporating most of the Normandy losses until the September 1944 tally.) As can be seen, StuG losses in the summer were only about a quarter of German losses in the summer fighting, but about half in the fall fighting.

| German AFV losses in the West in 1944 | | | | |
|---|---|---|---|---|
| | **Panzer** | Sturmgeschütz | Panzerjäger | Total |
| June–September 1944 | 1,941 | 663 | 253 | 2,857 |
| (percentage of total) | 68 | 23 | 9 | |
| October–November 1944 | 160 | 203 | 55 | 418 |
| (percentage of total) | 38 | 49 | 13 | |

The assault guns continued to play a central role in the fighting through the end of the war. German tank strength in the West increased in December 1944 with the sudden influx of Panzer divisions from the high command reserve to take part in the Ardennes attack. Once the Ardennes offensive was defeated at the end of December 1944, Hitler began to withdraw tank strength to the Eastern Front to deal with the Red Army's forthcoming January 1945 offensive. German tank strength in the West continued to decline through the remaining months of the war, with StuG III and Jagdpanzer 38(t) serving as the backbone for the increasingly depleted Panzer force.

| German AFV balance in the West, 1944–45 | | | | |
|---|---|---|---|---|
| Campaign | Panzer | Sturmgeschütz | Panzerjäger | Total |
| Normandy, July 1944 | 1,710 | 455 | 220 | 2,385 |
| (percentage of total) | 72 | 19 | 9 | |
| Ardennes, December 16, 1944 | 725 | 445 | 210 | 1,380 |
| (percentage of total) | 53 | 32 | 15 | |
| Defense of Rhine, February 5, 1945 | 390 | 925 | 110 | 1,425 |
| (percentage of total) | 27 | 65 | 8 | |
| Defense of Reich, April 28, 1945 | 60 | 170 | 80 | 310 |
| (percentage of total) | 19 | 55 | 26 | |

In contrast to the German case at Übach-Palenberg, tank destroyers were a much smaller fraction of the American armored force in the battle. Of the approximately 320 armored vehicles in "Cowboy Pete" Corlett's XIX Corps at the start of the battle, about 200 were M4 medium tanks, over 50 were M5A1 light tanks, and about 70 were M10 tank destroyers – less than a quarter of the force.

The US Army in the ETO maintained a relatively constant balance between its tanks and tank destroyers through the course of the campaign without the wildly fluctuating deployments seen in the Wehrmacht. Tank destroyers represented about 18 percent of the AFV inventory in Normandy in June 1944, and about 16 percent by the end of the war in May 1945. The technical composition of the force shifted through time due to the replacement of the M10 3in GMC with the M36 90mm GMC, so that the M10 force shrank from about three-quarters (77 percent) of the tank-destroyer fleet in the ETO in June 1944 to about one-quarter (23 percent) in May 1945.

| US M10 tank destroyer strength and losses in the ETO | | | | | | | | | | | | | |
|---|---|---|---|---|---|---|---|---|---|---|---|---|---|
| Strength* | 6/44 | 7/44 | 8/44 | 9/44 | 10/44 | 11/44 | 12/44 | 1/45 | 2/45 | 3/45 | 4/45 | 5/45 | |
| M10 | 691 | 743 | 758 | 763 | 486 | 573 | 790 | 768 | 686 | 684 | 427 | 427 | |
| M36 | 0 | 0 | 0 | 0 | 170 | 183 | 236 | 365 | 826 | 684 | 1,054 | 1,029 | |
| Total | 691 | 743 | 758 | 763 | 656 | 756 | 1,026 | 1,133 | 1,512 | 1,368 | 1,481 | 1,456 | |
| Losses | 6/44 | 7/44 | 8/44 | 9/44 | 10/44 | 11/44 | 12/44 | 1/45 | 2/45 | 3/45 | 4/45 | 5/45 | Total |
| M10 | 1 | 17 | 28 | 40 | 71 | 45 | 62 | 69 | 106 | 27 | 37 | 37 | 540 |
| M36 | 0 | 0 | 0 | 0 | 2 | 5 | 21 | 26 | 18 | 21 | 34 | 25 | 152 |
| Total | 1 | 17 | 28 | 40 | 73 | 50 | 83 | 95 | 124 | 48 | 71 | 62 | 692 |

*As of 20th of each month

As can be seen from the accompanying chart, the M10 battalions during the Aachen fighting had a very similar ammunition expenditure to that of the German StuG III units, with non-armored targets being much commoner than enemy tanks. Of the 2,380 rounds fired during this week of combat, only 13 percent were armor-piercing and most of these were fired against pillboxes and not German AFVs. More than three-fifths (>60 percent) of the engagements saw the M10s being used as self-propelled artillery and employing indirect fire.

| 802nd TD Battalion records, October 2–9, 1944 | | | | | | | | | |
|---|---|---|---|---|---|---|---|---|---|
| | Oct 2 | Oct 3 | Oct 4 | Oct 5 | Oct 6 | Oct 7 | Oct 8 | Oct 9 | Total |
| M10 operational | 31 | 29 | 28 | 29 | 30 | 28 | 29 | 30 | |
| M10 disabled | 2 | 3 | 5 | | | | | | |
| Enemy pillbox knocked out | 1 | 4 | 3 | 2 | 1 | 11 | | | |
| Enemy machine-gun nest knocked out | 3 | 2 | 2 | 7 | | | | | |
| Enemy AFV knocked out | 1 | 1 | 2 | | | | | | |
| Ammo, direct fire (AP+HE) | 151+211 | 0+18 | 117+95 | 13+102 | 19+31 | 15+111 | 5+46 | 0+2 | 936 (320+616) |
| Ammo, indirect fire (HE) | 183 | 176 | 340 | 224 | 311 | 210 | 1,444 | | |

The records for the 702nd TD Battalion present a slightly different picture since the battalion saw more AFV fighting. During the fighting in early October, the battalion claimed to have knocked out eight self-propelled guns and tanks, three towed antitank guns, five pillboxes, one observation post, and one artillery piece. A survey of 39 US Army tank-destroyer battalions after the war found that they had claimed to have destroyed 1,344 German AFVs during the 1944–45 ETO campaign for an

average of 34; the highest-scoring battalion claimed 105. The majority of targets were other types, including 684 antitank guns and field guns, 1,935 wheeled vehicles, 668 pillboxes, 614 machine-gun nests, and 18 aircraft.

The Übach-Palenberg battle also provides some insight into the relative value of different types of armored battalions in providing divisional support. Although US doctrine in 1944 did not permanently attach these battalions to specific divisions, in actual practice some battalions were essentially organic to particular divisions during the ETO campaign and so are characterized as such in this discussion. The XIX Corps included four varieties of supporting armored battalions: an organic tank battalion (743rd Tank Battalion, 30th Division); an organic towed tank-destroyer battalion (823rd TD Battalion, 30th Division), an organic self-propelled tank-destroyer battalion (702nd TD Battalion, 2nd Armored Division) and an attached self-propelled tank-destroyer battalion (803rd TD Battalion, 30th Division).

Of these four varieties of units, the organic tank battalion proved to be by far the most combat-effective. While it may seem an odd metric to employ in assessing combat effectiveness, the extent of vehicle losses provides one way to gauge the amount of combat in which the unit was engaged. There has been some tendency in recent historical writing to presume that severe tank losses in combat were somehow the "fault" of the unit and evidence of their poor performance. But in the type of combat seen in the Übach-Palenberg battle, heavy tank losses were inevitable due to the volume of enemy antitank fire and the difficulty of maneuvering in close-grain terrain with dense enemy defenses. In these circumstances, tank losses can be more properly viewed as "expenditure"; tank casualties both to enemy action and mechanical breakdown were inevitable. During this battle, the 743rd Tank Battalion strength had

StuG-Brig 280 fought against British and Canadian forces in the Netherlands in 1944–45, and this shows three of its assault guns at the end of the war. The brigade was unusual in that two of its batteries had been re-equipped with old StuG III fitted with the short L/24 gun as seen to the left. The nearest StuG III Ausf G has 16 "kill" markings on its barrel and the names "Mitzi" and "Erika" on the bow, while the middle vehicle, 223, has 18 kill markings.
(LAC PA-168903)

Some old StuG III Ausf C and Ausf D with the short L/24 gun that had been retired to training schools were put back into combat in the desperate days of 1945, such as this vehicle that was captured by Czech insurgents during the Prague uprising in May 1945. (Author's collection)

fallen from 57 M4 medium tanks on October 1 to 32 operational tanks with 25 tanks in repair on October 10. Actual losses had been about ten tanks lost and nine damaged by enemy action. The reason for this high rate of attrition in the unit was its extensive use in the fighting. The 743rd Tank Battalion took an active role every day and in nearly every major skirmish. The 30th Division had come to depend on the battalion to provide fire support during its missions, and this is evident in its after-action report where the battalion was in the thick of the fighting every day of the battle.

On the opposite end of the effectiveness spectrum was the 823rd TD Battalion, the organic towed battalion of the 30th Division. It played a minor role in the fighting and was used primarily to reinforce the divisional artillery. Its casualties were very modest since it did not see much direct combat. This unit had an exemplary record, and was very famous for its defensive actions at Mortain earlier in the summer. However, towed tank-destroyer units were simply not very useful in offensive combat no matter how determined the troops, and this is very evident in the unremarkable performance of this battalion in the Übach-Palenberg battle.

Of the remaining two self-propelled M10 battalions, the organic battalion, the 702nd TD Battalion with the 2nd Armored Division, had a more impressive record in the fighting. It lost four M10 tank destroyers in direct combat but at the same time knocked out far more German targets than did the 803rd TD Battalion. It appears repeatedly in the after-action reports of the combat commands. Once again, the reason for this discrepancy was in the greater amount of close combat in which the battalion was engaged. As an organic unit that had been serving with the division since the start of the Normandy campaign, the divisional commanders had a far better appreciation for the strength and weakness of the M10 tank destroyers and used them appropriately.

The division appreciated the firepower of the tank destroyers, and often used them in the advance guard of the task forces to deal with any German tank threat. Likewise, they knew that M10 tank destroyers were very vulnerable to mortar and artillery fire if left in static defensive positions in the front lines, and so avoided this mistake.

The 803rd TD Battalion was a corps-level asset and had bounced around between multiple divisions in Normandy without gaining much combat experience. Although the unit had a good record, its success or failure depended on the ability of its assigned division to handle it in an effective manner. The 30th Division had been assigned a towed tank-destroyer battalion since Normandy and was familiar with its limitations. As a result, the division tended to use the newly assigned battalion in a similar fashion, with more than half of its ammunition expended in indirect artillery missions rather than in direct-fire close-combat missions. The 30th Division used the 803rd TD Battalion in a much more tentative fashion than their organic 743rd Tank Battalion.

# THE POSTWAR JUDGMENT

It is not surprising that both the StuG III and M10 had serious design shortcomings since they were developed in the early days of combined-arms warfare and there was a technology–tactics mismatch when tactics evolved. Neither the StuG III nor the M10 3in GMC proved to be ideal combat vehicles in 1944 and 1945. Although they were often used to excellent effect by determined crews, this was frequently in spite of their design rather than because of the inherent combat effectiveness of their configuration.

The clearest judgment on their design came in the postwar years. The US Army completely abandoned the entire tank-destroyer concept as a technical and tactical mistake. As Jacob Devers had pointed out in 1943, "The best opponent of a tank is another tank." Tank battalions became the principal means for infantry close-combat support in Korea and for the early decades of the Cold War. The US Army toyed with the idea of lightly armored tank destroyers such as the M50 Ontos and M56 Scorpion, but these were more aberrations than mainstream concepts. Technology made gun-armed tank destroyers irrelevant with the advent of guided antitank missiles.

There was a strong break in tradition between the Wehrmacht of World War II and the Bundeswehr of the Cold War years. Germany did not begin designing its own armored vehicles again until a decade after the end of World War II. The classic assault-gun configuration disappeared, though a shadow of it could be seen in the Jagdpanzer Kanone 90mm of 1960. This used a fixed casemate like the StuG III, but it was intended from the outset as a tank destroyer, not an infantry-support gun. Its ancestry can be more closely tied to the wartime Panzerjäger such as the Jagdpanzer IV.

# BIBLIOGRAPHY

Books on the StuG III are much more numerous than those about the M10 tank destroyer. The two-volume Müller and Zimmermann study offers the most detailed history of the design and manufacture of the StuG III, while the two-volume Laugier account provides the most in-depth operational history.

Coverage of the combat record of the StuG III in the West is not as detailed as for the Eastern Front units. The combat account of the fighting north of Aachen was prepared using archival records. The US National Archives and Records Administration in College Park, Maryland has the war diary (*Kriegstagbuch*) of the LXXXI. Armeekorps, which includes extensive annexes on unit strength. The Heichler study is the most thorough account of German operations in English, and the G-2 records for the 30th Division and 2nd Armored Division were also consulted regarding German units in the Aachen fighting. The US side of the battle was prepared using the after-action reports for the US units including the 117th and 119th Infantry Regiments of 30th Division, the 743rd Tank Battalion, the 702nd, 803rd, and 823rd TD battalions, and the 66th and 67th Armored regiments of the 2nd Armored Division. Another source on tank-destroyer performance in Italy and the ETO is the collection of the US Army Ground Forces Observer Board, which issued short reports on lessons learned from observation trips to the combat zones.

## US GOVERNMENT PUBLICATIONS

Denny, Bryan, *The Evolution and Demise of US Tank Destroyer Doctrine in the Second World War*, Command and General Staff College, 2003

FM 18-15, *Tank Destroyer Drill and Crew Drill*, December 4, 1943

FM 18-20, *Tactical Employment of Tank Destroyer Platoon Self-Propelled*, May 9, 1944

Gabel, Christopher, *Seek, Strike, and Destroy: US Army Tank Destroyer Doctrine in World War II*, Command and General Staff College, 1985

General Board, US Forces, European Theater, *Organization, Equipment and Tactical Employment of Tank Destroyer Units* (Study No. 60), 1945

Historical Section, Army Ground Forces, *Tank Destroyer History* (Study No. 29), 1945


## US ARMY FOREIGN MILITARY STUDIES

Hechler, Lucian, *The Germans Opposite XIX Corps*, Report R-21, 1953

Lange, Wolfgang, *183. Volksgrenadier Division Sep 1944–25 Jan 1945*, Report B-753, 1949

Macholz, Siegfried, *49. Infanterie Division*, Report B-792, 1948


## BOOKS

Bailey, Charles, *Faint Praise: American Tanks and Tank Destroyers during World War II*, Archon Books (North Haven, CT, 1983)

Doyle, Hilary & Jentz, Tom, *Sturmgeschütz III & IV*, New Vanguard 37, Osprey Publishing (Oxford, 2001)

Feist, Uwe & Fleischer, Wolfgang, *Sturmgeschütz*, Ryton (Bellingham, WA:, 1998)

Folkestad, William, *The View from the Turret: The 743rd Tank Battalion during World War II*, White Mane (Shippensburg, PA, 1996)

Gill, Lonnie, *Tank Destroyer Forces – WWII*, Turner (Nashville, TN, 1992)

Hewitt, Robert, *Workhorse of the Western Front: The Story of the 30th Infantry Division*, Infantry Journal Press (Washington, DC, 1946)

Kurowski, Frank, *Sturmgeschütz vor: Assault Guns to the Front*, J. J. Fedorowicz (Winnipeg, 1999)

Laugier, Didier, *Sturmartillerie* (two volumes), Heimdal (Bayeux, 2011)

Muller, Peter and Zimmermann, Wolfgang, *Sturmgeschütz III: Development, Production, Deployment* (two volumes), History Facts (Andelfingen, 2009)

Spielberger, Walter, *Sturmgeschütz & Its Variants*, Schiffer (Atglen, PA, 1993)

Yeide, Harry, *The Tank Killers: A History of America's World War II Tank Destroyer Force*, Casemate )Havertown, PA, 2007)

Zaloga, Steven J., *M10 and M36 Tank Destroyers 1942–53*, New Vanguard 57, Osprey Publishing (Oxford, 2002)

Zaloga, Steven J., *US Tank and Tank Destroyer Battalions in the ETO 1944–45*, Battle Orders 10, Osprey Publishing (Oxford, 2005)

# INDEX